IMMIGRANT
AMERICAN

LIVING AN AMERICAN LIFE WITH AFRICAN PERSPECTIVES

YVES BATOBA

Outskirts Press, Inc.
http://www.outskirtspress.com

Paperback ISBN: 978-1-9772-4693-6
Hardback ISBN: 978-1-9772-4713-1

Outskirts Press and the "OP" logo are trademarks belonging to Outskirts Press, Inc.

PRINTED IN THE UNITED STATES OF AMERICA

To Mami and Papa,
You are the best parents I could have ever asked for.
Thank you for all you have done for our family.

To Christia Dawn,
Giving you my last name is the best decision I ever
made. You are truly the GREATEST OF ALL TIME.

Table of Contents

1. Son of Zaire 1

2. African American or American African? 9

3. Eat the Fufu With Your Hands 20

4. Tap Into Those Genetics 26

5. The River and the Reservoir 34

6. Good Internet for Your Soul 45

7. Jesus of Nazareth, Texas.. 52

8. The Color is Deep.. 59

9. American Dream Remixed 67

10. The Lion Speaks Back 76

11. The Dawn of Yves.. 89

12. Intercultural Love... 98

1

SON OF ZAIRE

I AM FROM a country that no longer exists. Well... kind of. On the 30th of June 1960, what was formerly known as The Belgian Congo achieved its independence from Belgium. It did this under the leadership of the great Congolese politician Patrice Lumumba before he got assassinated (in 2002, Belgium formally apologized for its role played in the assassination). Since then, the country has gone by multiple names. The Republic of Congo was the country's name for the first five years of its inception. This is not to be confused with another neighboring country which also chose the same name upon achieving its independence from France. Then, a constitutional referendum in 1965 resulted in the country's official name being changed to the "Democratic Republic of the Congo." The country I was born in was birthed when the then President Mobutu renamed it again in 1971 to "Republic of Zaire."

Between 1971 and 1997, Republic of Zaire was the second largest country in all of sub-Saharan Africa, following closely behind Sudan, and was the 11th largest in the world. Zaire was also host of what has been called "arguably the greatest sporting event of the 20th century." This happened when undefeated world heavyweight champion George Foreman was overthrown by Muhammad Ali in a historic boxing event known as *The Rumble in the Jungle* – it was the world's most-watched live television broadcast at the time. Zaire had a lot of promise, one that was fueled by a great desire to rid itself of the lingering vestiges of Belgian colonialism and the continuing influence of Western culture. All of these goals were in order to create a more centralized and singular national identity. Despite being home to natural resources which had vast potential, and also having massive mineral wealth, the country was characterized by widespread cronyism, corruption and economic mismanagement. Zaire eventually collapsed in 1997. This occurred amid the destabilization in the eastern parts of the country, following the aftermath of the Rwandan genocide; all of which saw an increase in ethnic violence in the First Congo War.

My family was living in the nation's capital, Kinshasa, when the military troops reached the city in the middle of May 1997, just two months before my 6th birthday. We lived in a beautiful house in Congo. When you entered through the black gates, in front, there was a long driveway which led to a garage for the cars, or, you could veer to the left and incoming guests could park their cars in the big courtyard. Just past the courtyard, there was a large grass field where we kept a swing set which we would frequently go out to play with. Every once in a while, there would be a goat and some chickens in the field that the workers eventually cooked. Friends and family frequently visited and generally, the house carried great ambience. Life was good for us in Congo until the day we started hearing the sounds of bombs exploding and those of machine guns firing.

The war was approaching us.

It was during this time that signaled a change in all that we knew for our family. At the time, I had four siblings and all of us were visiting my Uncle Para and Aunt Louise in Brazzaville, which was just across the Congo River in the neighboring Republic of Congo. We felt pretty safe in the neighborhood where we lived but, for our safety, my parents thought it best that we stayed in Brazzaville until things became calmer in Kinshasa. By the middle of June 1997, things soon became worse while we were there. Before we knew it, we too could hear those same gun fires and explosions where we stayed. In fact, we were worse off in Brazzaville than we were in Kinshasa. And so, we had to go back.

The only problem was that in order to reach the boat that could take us across the Congo River and back to Kinshasa, we had to go through the actual war zone and in the process, risk our lives. According to the news on television, it said there were people making it to the boats every single day. A family friend however came to the house to tell Uncle Para that houses nearby were being bombed, and the house we stayed in was likely to be destroyed soon. We then had two choices. We could stay where we were at and be killed or captured, or, we could take a 50/50 chance at survival by placing ourselves right into the fire. There were eleven of us in total staying at the house. We found ourselves sleeping underneath the dining room table. An act we did just to avoid the possibility of being hurt in case a bullet came down from the roof. My uncle also put a mattress on top of the dining room table. It was to serve as an extra layer of impact just in case the worst happened.

Some of us had to sleep under chairs placed side by side primarily so they could cover our entire body. My oldest sister, Lydie, who was 14 at the time, was so worried about us leaving all of our clothes and other belongings behind. Typical teenager. Still, there were so many of us carrying all types of concerns about the situation, some simply more serious than others. We were all mainly undecided on whether or not to attempt fleeing. This was until early one morning when my other big sister, Patricia, woke up to a bullet on the ground which lay about four feet away from her head. When Uncle Para saw that, there was no other decision to be taken. We were leaving that very morning.

We packed as much as we could carry and although bombs and guns were going off around us, we still walked. When someone yelled for us to hit the ground, we too hit the ground and crawled as if we belonged in the army. When it was time we got back on our exhausted feet; we continued to walk.

And walk.....and crawl.....and walk.....and crawl.....and walk.

We walked the entire day, surrounded by what seemed like thousands and thousands of people. A lot of the mothers marching had their babies attached to their backs using a kanga. Kangas are large rectangular cloths which feature a colorful design on the fabric. Mothers usually wrap kangas around their bodies similar to a towel to help carry their babies on their backs. They roll up the material on their chests and tie the loose ends while the babies are tightly secured. Laetitia, my little 4-year-old sister, was kept in a kanga on Aunt Louise's back. At one point while we were walking, some soldiers ran up to them and pulled them into a room where people were being shot at a point blank distance. Conflict existed between Congolese people from Kinshasa and Congolese people from Brazzaville and in that room, people from Kinshasa were randomly shot.

Because Aunt Louise and Uncle Para had lived in Brazzaville for years, somebody who was in the room recognized who they were and screamed at the soldiers, "Do not shoot them, she is one of us!"

That made the soldiers release them and they rejoined the rest of us as we kept on marching. That random person saved all their lives. For so many people walking on that trail, theirs was not the case. My big brother, Lionel, later told me about a baby that he saw, that was sitting up next to his mother's wounded corpse, just crying.

"I thought about grabbing the baby so that it could come with us," Lionel added as he recounted the stories to me years later. "But I was 8 years old and I did not want to get left behind. I had to keep going," he said.

After about 13 or 14 hours of marching, we finally reached a Catholic convent where lots of people took refuge. We stayed at the convent, a place we all sat and slept on its floor for two days and two nights. The whole time there, we ate a lot of spam and tried to keep each other's spirits up. During those nights, we were seated around each other and laughing; I cannot remember what jokes were being told, but I know there was laughter, spam, and an air of uncertainty. On the morning of the third day, a man who was talking on a walkie talkie, approached us and said that word had gotten to my parents that we had made it through the war zone. My dad was able to send money to enable us board one of the canoes going across the Congo River. Because none of us could swim, it made the entire canoe ride a terrifying one for all eleven of us. Just about everybody on the canoe was deep in prayer, making all types of promises to God that they would keep if He could just ensure we were alive and made it safely across.

By the grace of God, all our prayers were answered and we indeed arrived on the other side of the Congo River. Upon reaching Kinshasa, we were met by so many of our family members on the border who were basking and full of rejoice. My parents' faces looked as though they were seeing ghosts. Every single person around us bawled tears of joy and gratitude. After hours of walking, crawling underneath bullets, seeing dozens of bodies drop dead around us, and even almost losing my little sister and aunt, the Lord had spared all of our lives. My mother did not know if she would still have other children. We would later find out that ironically, my mom was pregnant that day.

Glory to God, now, forever and always.

As we taxied back to our house, I noticed that the city was still buzzing. Despite all of the imminent chaos, people were still out working, hustling, buying, and selling in order to feed their families. It felt like the same old Zaire, but only that the country had a different name. Kinshasa, the capital, had been captured by Laurent-Desire Kabila, who took over the country's government as President and changed its name from Zaire to the Democratic Republic of Congo. I was the son of Zaire, but I came back to the DRC. Those same war sounds – gunfire and explosions – were still there and showed us that there were no signs of peace returning any time soon. With my mother pregnant with my little brother, Nathan, we all knew that our growing family needed to do something different.

The invasion that came with the First Congo War caused my family and many other Congolese families to flee away from the misery. Some left for Europe, others left for other African nations, and we also heard of a few who were leaving for the United States of America. We knew that South Africa had recently formed a democratic government with Nelson Mandela elected as its President. The country seemed promising. So Dad, Mom, Lydie, Patricia, Lionel, myself Yves, Laetitia, and our newborn Nathan all left our war-torn country in the summer of 1998 and flew to the city of Johannesburg, South Africa.

Even though apartheid had ended, we did not realize at first, that there was still so much racial tension in the air. We moved into an area of town where we were one of a few black families living there. Even with institutional racial segregation being outlawed four years prior to our moving, we were however met with resentment and violence. The white people in South Africa did not like us because of the color of our skin. Ironically, the black people native to the country also did not like us because we were not South African.

When I started attending school there, it was that Fall and I was in the second grade. I also did not have any friends at my new school. My teacher, Ms. Briganda, was the first white lady whom I had as a teacher. She was a sweet, mild-mannered woman in her early 20's who came up to me occasionally to inform me to go to the Principal's office and meet with Lionel and Laetitia because something had happened at home. There were a couple of times that our house got broken into and invaded by burglars. On different occasions, people also approached my mother and threatened Nathan's life if we refused moving. Another time, we came home early to see my mother with a black eye and a bruised lip, which came from an attack by a group of burglars who had broken in.

Johannesburg existed in a blur. All I remember from that period is that I absolutely hated living there. It was the first time in my life that I had extended relations with people of a different race. It was the first time too that made me wonder why people hated us for things which were completely out of our control. Things such as the color of our skin. We held a family meeting and decided that living in Johannesburg was too unbearable for us to stay. It seemed too, like things were calming down back home in Kinshasa. Based on what we saw on the news channels; it was safer than it was when we left. So we all moved back.

Back to the Democratic Republic of Congo, the newly formed country.

We came to find out however, that the conflict did not calm down; it just was not reported outside of the country. In fact, the bloodshed had become even more aggressive. The new government had ordered the Congolese military to arrest and kill anyone who was of the Tutsi tribe, most of whom were Rwandese and Ugandan. Some of these people included many of my parents' friends and former co-workers. On one occasion, some of their Rwandese friends even slept over at our house as they tried to dodge persecution. That's my parents' attitude – always wanting to be helpful, even in the face of life threatening danger.

With all the ongoing chaos, we had a family meeting to decide where we should move. We knew that although we did not like being in South Africa, it was way safer there than being amongst the political instability of Congo. We brought up the issue with some distant family members who were living near Dallas, Texas. The United States of America… the land of opportunity. We had previously seen images of the Statue of Liberty, Hollywood, and Disney World on our television. The thought of living there soon excited us. We made up our minds. We were moving to America!

Months after that family meeting, the Batoba family went to the airport with one-way tickets bound for the United States. While we were at the airport, armed policemen marched up to my parents and stopped them from moving further. "That's them! They are the ones who helped the Tutsi escape!" the policemen said. We all didn't know what was happening. They separated the kids and sent us back home while they kept my parents at the airport.

They arrested my mom and dad and threw them into separate jails. The next day my dad was interrogated by the police. He was given this statement: "Mr. Batoba you cannot leave the country because you have been accused of helping Déogratias Bugera flee the country." My father was then put on a no-fly list due to suspicions of helping Bugera, a high-ranking government official whom my father had never even met. Meanwhile, my mother was kept in a women's prison with other women accused of political crimes and was forced to clean toilets and sweep the large courtyard. Four days in jail. That was how long they were kept. Every day, large jeeps were loaded with prisoners who were taken to a camp to be killed. On the fourth day, my parents too were scheduled to be killed.

My dad made a phone call to Francois Beya, a friend of his who was a national security advisor. Mr. Beya, was able to get my parents out of the jails just before it was their turn to be taken on the large jeeps. For the next three months, my family lived as refugees staying with different nuns and priests; until we were able to finally attain fake passports from a family who lived in the Ivory Coast. These passports already came with U.S. visas and they were what allowed us to enter the United States on July 11, 1999; just three days before my 8th birthday. Once we were settled in the state of Texas, we applied for the right of political asylum. After that, we were granted refugee status and protection from the United States of America.

At eight years old, the son of Zaire became himself, an Immigrant American.

2 | AFRICAN AMERICAN OR AMERICAN AFRICAN?

UPON ARRIVING IN Texas, I remember my parents, uncles, and other members of the Congolese community continually telling me not to become influenced by the Black Americans. Then, there were unpleasant preconceived notions about African Americans, springing up mainly due to their portrayal in the media. For example, the 1990's saw the incarceration rates in America shoot through the roof. It was more apparent in the Black community due to a system of public policies, institutional practices, cultural representation, and other norms which all work to reinforce racial inequality. We (African Immigrants) saw this stuff on our television screens without realizing that all of it was a result of structural racism.

The criminal justice system in the United States, is perhaps the clearest example of structural racism in the country. The US has the highest incarceration rate in the world – of which an overwhelming burden of contact with the system discriminates against communities of color, especially those who are African Americans.

I once remember watching the 1993 American crime movie Sugar Hill, in which Wesley Snipes and Michael Wright both played the roles of two brothers who were major drug dealers in Harlem, a New York City neighborhood. There is a scene in the movie, where they wanted to do business with two Nigerian men, but one of the Nigerians said to them: "I'm sorry, but we cannot work with akata." When Wesley Snipes' character asked him what "akata" meant, the Nigerian man replied "Black American...Cotton Picker." Snipes' character then proceeded to head-butt the Nigerian and threw him on the ground. It is a ridiculous thing that one even thinks that way because countries all over Africa were colonized by white Europeans and people from there were treated like "akata" too. Even when my family escaped the war and went to South Africa, the Dutch people had evident prejudice towards the original Africans that was still very much existing. So much so, that they did not even want to live amongst them.

When I was living in Africa, whether that was in Kinshasa or Johannesburg, Black Americans were often portrayed even on the continent in a negative light on television; again we just didn't know that it was a result of structural racism. It was not until a few years later, that I would learn about laws which acted as an instrument of oppression. Laws whose implementation were advantageous not just to white Americans, but also European immigrants. I would later learn that African Americans who had been enslaved were promised 40 acres of land and a mule in order to jump start their new lives after being freed from bondage.

That promise never got fulfilled.

In fact, the only form of reparations that ever happened in reference to slavery in America, was when slave owners in Washington D.C. were paid as much as 300 dollars for each slave lost as a result of slaves being emancipated. Even affirmative action, which was created in the 60's, was marketed as a scheme created to right the wrong that was done to Black people. In reality, it ended up being one for ALL minorities, including even white women. White women as a group have benefited more from affirmative action than most black people have. In addition, since most white women usually marry white men, it can be said too that white families have benefited more from affirmative action than black families as a whole. We did not know about any of these things back in Africa. All we saw as Africans were the negative stereotypes associated with Black Americans.

Meanwhile in America, on the reverse, the only images people had of Africans, were African kids who were starving with flies on their faces or, they were packed in schools that had no books. Both portrayals were very small illustrations of life that made it appear to both parties as though there existed a monumental difference between black folks in North America and black folks living in Africa. One of the biggest differences, however, is that the original heritage of black Americans became erased when their ancestors were captured, enslaved and brought to this foreign country. More recent black migrants coming to the US may know and be proud of their heritage; the United States' legacy of slavery however means that even they will face challenges such as racism that non-Black immigrants may not face.

My immigrant family had to adjust to the reality of becoming an ethnic minority for the first time when we came to live in the United States. Most Black immigrants come from countries of origin in Africa or the Caribbean, where they often are in the racial majority. I will say that if there was any prejudice given towards us, it felt a lot subtler than what we experienced in South Africa. In South Africa, it was the first time I remember facing obvious discrimination based simply on my physical features. That experience was traumatic and also prevented me from trusting most non-black people I encountered later on in the United States.

Mom and Dad never once looked down on African-Americans unlike other African immigrants had been manipulated to do, but instead, they made sure to explain that our priorities as immigrants were different. Black Americans are actually some of the most welcoming people I have ever been around as a person. I have noticed from being around them, that they welcome just about any group into their communities and ensure to support the businesses that these groups in question set up especially in Black neighborhoods. What has been interesting to observe however, has been how my parents have evolved in their thinking over the years. Maybe it is because of the restitution of African culture which is springing up in the United States today – African Americans for example are proudly tracing their ancestry, unapologetically wearing African garments and are beginning to find strength in their African roots.

But this is the reality: Whether you are African, Caribbean, or American, when you come over to the U.S., the general public just groups all of us as Black. The subject of our previous identity does not matter where we were previously from. Most of the public discussion of immigration in the United States focuses almost entirely on Latinx immigration; thereby overlooking the 4.2 million Black immigrants currently in the country and ignoring the existence and diversity of Black immigrants altogether.

My siblings and I often hid that we were African and tried to assimilate into the predominant culture. This was a direct response to us not wanting to feel ostracized, as we had been in South Africa. When people asked us where we were from, because we spoke French, we said we came from Paris, France. What a horrible way to exist! We were hiding our true identity because of fear ironically in what is considered the freest nation on the planet.

My best friend in 3rd grade was a kid named Malek who was from Sudan. Malek had the darkest skin I had ever seen. Like me, he had just moved to the United States and we took ESL classes together at school and we lived in apartment complexes next to each other. Normally after school, we rode the school bus back to our apartments, checked in with our parents before then meeting up outside to play. Every now and then, other neighborhood kids would join us – Michael, Carlos, Qais, and Miles. They were White, Mexican, Arabic, and, yes, also Black American kids. Malek was the African kid and I was the "French" kid. Every time I stepped outside to play was an opportunity in getting a real first-hand multicultural experience of America. That experience completely changed for me, when my family moved from Irving to the suburbs of Keller, TX.

My world became a lot less diverse when we moved houses to Keller. I became one of the few people in my city who was not white. According to U.S. Census data when I moved to Keller, at the time, there were 27,388 people that lived in the town – 25,676 were white and only 392 of us were Black. In Irving, my teacher was Black; in Keller however, there wasn't a single Black teacher in Willis Lane Elementary School. I was so sad to leave all of my friends in Irving, especially Malek, but I was excited about making new ones as well.

Laetitia and I showed up to school on our first day wearing our school uniforms from our old school. We looked around and saw that everyone else was dressed in regular attire. Our minds lit up at the idea that we could come to school dressed how we wanted for the very first time in our lives. "This is like how they dress to school in the movies," Laetitia said to me.

Adjusting to life in Keller in the 4th grade was more seamless. I didn't really give much thought to the fact that I was the only Black kid in my class. All I knew was that I had to get good grades and also had to stay up to date with the latest Pokémon episodes or else, my new friends, Anthony and Landon, would spoil it for me at recess. When I was taught social studies at school, I learned about some of the great historical white men and women. During Black History Month, we'd learn about slavery but the teachers would give us a watered down lesson about civil rights activists such as Martin Luther King, Jr., Malcolm X, and Rosa Parks. Come to think of it though, the teachers themselves were probably never educated about the great Black historical figures in America such as Frederick Douglas, Thurgood Marshall, or Madam C.J. Walker.

I didn't know any better at the time myself. All of it felt to me like the normal American experience. When I went to my friends' houses, we listened to rock bands like Smash Mouth or Blink-182 or, their parents played country songs by George Strait or Brad Paisley. I was fully immersed and was living in the suburban, white American experience of the 2000's. There was rock and roll music, going to skate parks with my skateboard, and watching Boy Meets World episodes on the Disney Channel.

Meanwhile in my house, we often hosted our Congolese friends and family to still get a little taste of Africa for ourselves. All of it felt like a good balance to me.

Around 2002, when I was going into the 6th grade, Razor scooters became a must-have for kids. These were even more popular than bicycles, and all the kids in my neighborhood rode the kick scooters. When my parents got me one during Christmas, I spent all my time out in the street learning new tricks and riding around with some of the other neighborhood kids. There was one time in particular when I was out riding scooters, where I came across my classmate Grant.

Grant was the first person my age who I remember having a deep voice and a mustache. I knew him from school, but I hardly saw him outside of school. I went up to him and the two of us ended up spending the next few hours together, just hanging out and teaching each other new tricks. Towards the end of the day, I remember Grant said to me: "I like Black people. It's just annoying when they're TOO Black, you know? Like the way they talk too Black and the cornrows, and stuff like that. I like you because you're Black but not TOO Black."

Was that not an absolutely preposterous and offensive thing for one to say, right?! The craziest part however, is that my 11-year-old brain took that ridiculous statement as a compliment. Hindsight now is 20/20 and I can fully admit that then, I was brainwashed to think that there was a certain level of "Blackness" that I should have stayed away from. All of it could be traced back to us being warned about Black Americans when we had first moved to Texas. Whenever I saw Black male celebrities on TV, I saw the flashy medallion chains they wore, du-rags, tilted baseball caps, and I paid attention to how they communicated. African Americans were pioneering the hip-hop culture and I honestly loved everything about it: from the music, the fashion, the slang, and even the walk. Those looked more appealing to me than anything I had ever seen around Keller.

By the end of 6th grade, I had made friends with one of the other few Black students in my school. His name was Olivier and although his parents too were African immigrants, he had fully embraced the hip-hop culture in America. Befriending Olivier was a turning point in my 11-year-old life, because it allowed me to make a conscious decision. One that I would fully embrace this culture that I loved, even if it perpetuated stereotypes that would make me seem "too Black" in the eyes of people like Grant. If any of my peers did not accept me because of that choice, then I wouldn't want to be friends with them anyway. Olivier and I played football together, rode our bikes around town together, and we bonded over Ludacris, Nelly, and G-Unit.

My parents were fine with my becoming more "Americanized"; as long as my school work came first. To them, I wasn't more African American. I was just an American African. American was what described my personality, while the label African described my priorities. There is nothing that African parents love more than the ability to brag to other African parents, about how well their kids are doing in their schools. There is a joke in African immigrant circles that says that kids usually have one of four career options when they grow up in an African home. They are:
1) Doctor
2) Lawyer
3) Engineer
4) Disgrace to the Family

I was the first of the Batoba kids to stop telling people I came from France. I just saw myself as Texan. It's not that I was ashamed of being African. At that point, I just identified more with America. Besides, people were not really asking where I was from because they already assumed that I was American. How were they supposed to know that I wasn't a U.S. citizen if I did not tell them? My older siblings still had a bit of an accent, but I sounded fully American. This was the same also for my younger siblings. I went from being totally immersed in the white, suburban lifestyle to being infatuated by the hip-hop culture in America. Before middle school ended, Olivier and his family had moved away to Canada. By then, I had had a great group of friends who fully accepted me for who I was. Ironically, this group was extremely diverse and we sometimes joked about how we represented the United Nations. We were Ricky, Fabian, Chris, Josh, Austin, Sam, Mooney, and John. Three of them were Mexican, Three were white, one was Asian, and another was mixed-race. Of the eight, five of them were either first or second generation immigrants from Mexico, and Great Britain. Then there was me who was from Congo.

Technology has allowed me to keep in touch with most of them even now as adults. The majority of our conversations back then revolved around typical teenage topics and concerns: girls, video games, sports, school, etc...

But for me, it was the way we joked around each other that stood out. Any and every stereotype that one can think of about our ethnic backgrounds were fair game. But we were all best friends and so we could separate a joke from someone's true feelings. If someone said something which seemed out of line, you had to come back with something even more out of line and we all would laugh about it after.

The politically correct and "cancel culture" world of the 2020's would have absolutely hated us! I am actually glad about the way social media has made it easier for us to hold people accountable for what they say, because now, we really do know better. Even though we probably knew better back then, we were completely influenced by the shock value employed in music, film, comedy, and television. During that time, it was all about how shocking you also could be AFTER you stepped – no, jumped – over the proverbial line.

I completely understand why young people in the 2020's get outraged by some of the content they see from the 1990's and late 2000's. As we have progressed in society and continually see how obstructive this type of content can be, social norms have also changed with it and I think we are better off as a people because of it. I always saw the value that came with having a diverse group of friends. I cannot trade lives with any of them and they too cannot trade their lives with mine, but our friendship always allowed us to have genuine conversations that provide more perspective.

Things started to change a bit in high school as students there began to form cliques. Among the cliques at Keller High School, there existed your group of preppy kids who wore all the latest fashions and had the new technology; the jocks whose entire social identity revolved around sports and related activities; the teacher's pets who excelled in school work and often befriended teachers; the loners who didn't really have friends and were content with being alone. I did not necessarily belong to any of these cliques, as I often found myself befriending just about every type of person in high school. I even went out of my way to also befriend the loners.

My unique life experience and interactions by the time I got to high school allowed me to have a great competency in managing interpersonal relationships. On any given day, I had to maneuver my way through multiple cultures. I woke up in one culture at home, communicated using a different culture when talking to my friends from Irving, and lived in a different culture when in Keller. It was natural for me. What some people call "code switching," I view instead as cross-culture capacity. The best part about growing up like this, is that it has allowed me to identify what is truly cultured and what is someone merely playing a character.

There was this other group I discovered in high school that I had not known existed in Keller... It was made up of mostly Black (and some Brown) students who just seemed to understand each other and could relate to being Black or Brown in a community where almost everybody else was white. It was almost as if we shared a collective identity and just understood it. There were plenty of things which we disagreed on, but we did not talk negatively about each other; especially not to anyone who was outside of that group.

It was a case of: "I know what you have been through and you know what I have been through without even saying it out loud."

I remember in 9th grade when I still spent most of my free time hanging with my diverse group of friends from middle school, there was a period of time in it where I thought that I just wasn't funny anymore. Each time I joked around, nobody laughed. I understood all their jokes, but all of mine went over their heads and they just didn't get it. This felt very discouraging, because humor is one of the things I value the most in a friendship. Well, when I went to school and started spending more time around this group of mostly Black students, not only were my jokes a hit amongst them, we often would go back and forth with jokes which kept flowing. It clicked in me then, that the similarity in our shared experiences are what led to the better humor. A joke is not funny when it has to be explained. It is also hard to explain something to someone who does not have years of experience and foreknowledge in that topic. It's like when a Black comedian makes a joke about having to exist in dual cultures. The Black audience would mostly get the joke, while the white audience mostly would not.

Naturally, the friends that I became closest to in high school came from this group of friends. Justin and Cesar were the main homies. Justin was a tall, skinny black kid whose mom came from Louisiana and dad, Maryland. Cesar on the other hand, was a short, skinny kid from southern California whose parents were Guatemalan immigrants. I had their backs and they too had mine. I could relate to them in a way that most of my other friends could not understand; this was especially when we needed to vent about some of the racially charged encounters we faced in Keller.

*Yves, with his friends Justin, Antone, and
Hajj in high school (left to right)*

3 | EAT THE FUFU WITH YOUR HANDS

THERE HAVE BEEN a lot of wars fought across the Congo of Africa, but I had never heard about the fierce rivalry which exists between Nigerians, Ghanaians, and Senegalese people until I was in my late 20's. My wife, Dawn and I were visiting my friend Daramola and his wife, Karen, at their high-rise apartment located in downtown Miami. Daramola is one of the nicest people I've ever met. He is originally from Nigeria and spent some time living in London and Mexico before finally moving to Miami. During our visit, his wife asked us, "Do you guys want to try some jollof rice?"

Of course we said yes. Jollof rice is one of the most popular dishes in Africa, but it is especially popular in West Africa. It is eaten at parties, naming ceremonies, weddings, funerals — you name it. At any gathering, a familiar and comforting pot of steaming jollof rice is always nearby. "We cooked it the Nigerian way," Daramola said to me as he scooped it out of the pot. I had heard previously that there were dozens of variations of jollof rice, all of which depended on where the person making it came from.

I jokingly told Daramola, "I heard the Ghanaian way is the best way to make it.

"Uh oh," said his wife Karen.

"How could you say something so insensitive and personal?" he replied.

I could not even tell if he was joking or not. Jollof rice is amazing, but it is also war – the type of the deliciously friendly variety.

My friends who are from the West Africa region, the continent, the African diaspora and beyond regularly engage in debates of which country prepares the best jollof rice! Typically, Jollof rice is cooked with tomato sauce with variations of seasonings, vegetables, oils, and grains of rice. The magic and difference happens in the way that it is prepared and blended. In 2014, the hashtag #JollofGate trended, when British celebrity chef Jamie Oliver advanced his own version, one containing coriander and cherry tomatoes. He was met by howling derision online from Africans, in a fleeting display of Pan-African unity.

"Try this and tell me if you have ever tasted anything better in life," Karen said to me with a smile on her face. I went back for more, and then some more, and then some more. To be honest, even then, I had never tasted a variation of Jollof rice that I did not like. After a night of hanging out with our friends, we put on our shoes to leave. As we headed towards the front door, Daramola had one more thing to say to us before we left.

"And make sure to tell your Ghanaian friends about how much you enjoyed the dish."

The debate about which country has the best rice is a light-hearted one of course, and my brothers and sisters who are from other countries get upset when I don't include them in the rivalry. This passionate bond over food is something I have always enjoyed seeing. Among Africans in the United States however, there seems to be more unity than with Africans living in the actual continent.

When my wife and I went on our honeymoon trip to Europe in the summer of 2019, we wanted to explore as many different dishes as we could. Paellas in Spain, wiener schnitzels in Germany, even escargot in France, were amongst many of the meals which we enjoyed. One thing that was obvious to us though, was the way we felt after we ate; or rather, the way we DIDN'T feel. There was no feeling of excessive bloating or gas, no fatigue, and no sluggishness. I remember telling my wife that I felt the same way as when I visited Congo in 2018 and on my mission trip to Kenya after college.

My friend Elliott is a farm and ranch aficionado from South Carolina who knows and researches all things related to agriculture. After he spent a couple of years living in Europe, we had a conversation about his experience and I asked him what he thought about the food there compared to that of the United States. He told me that all of it begins with the government regulations. Here's what is stated in the food safety section of the European Union's website for example:

The EU's food safety policy covers food from farm to fork. It is designed to guarantee:

- *safe, nutritious food & animal feed*
- *high standards of animal health & welfare & plant protection*
- *clear information on the origin, content/ labelling & use of food.*

"Every country in the European Union has restrictions or straight up bans on the production and sale of genetically modified foods," Elliott told me. He continued, "You can't even compare that to our oversized, chemically-injected, and pesticide-filled crops and livestock in the US. There is so much consumer demand that we risk losing nutritional value." So even when I'm eating African food that my mother made in the United States, while it tastes amazing, it still does not feel quite the same because she is using American produce to prepare it.

While growing up in America, it always felt to me as though the front door of our home was the "wood between the worlds." When I would get home from school and turn its doorknob, a delightful aroma of different herbs, spices, and sauces being prepared was what welcomed me in. The kitchen felt like it was Africa, and Africa at that point felt amazing. Nothing makes me feel more connected to my Congolese roots than eating some good Congolese food made by mom. By the way, I have never met ANYONE who makes Congolese food better than my mother. My favorite meal for example is Congolese cassava leaves, which is also known as "pondu" in Lingala; it is made with some lamb stew, and eaten with fufu on the side. A real Congolese person does not eat this using silverware either. I normally would wash my hands, cut some fufu with my hands and use that to collect the rest of the food on the plate. That's the way to eat it! That is, only when I was around my family.

The food which we ate at home looked completely different from anything that I saw at my friends' houses. I was also embarrassed to let my friends see it. The confines of the walls which we lived in was a sacred place. I could be my full African self while enjoying these meals and when I visited them, we could indulge in some hamburgers, pizza, or apple pies. When my mom knew that I was having friends over, she would cook some French fries, baked chicken, and make us a salad. She kept it familiar. As time went on, I became more comfortable in my true identity. Not only did I stop telling people that I spoke French because I was from France, but I also wanted my friends to become aware of the food, too. I still had that bad taste in my mouth from South Africa; that taste that made me feel I would be rejected simply because of my identity.

One day, my friend Chris and his older brother John came over to our house in Keller during summer break. They were of Mexican descent but had spent their entire lives in America, growing up just outside of Los Angeles, in California. We were all playing in the backyard when mom told us to come in because our food was ready. As I approached the dining table, I saw an interesting spread: one half were familiar American dishes, and the other half was made up of traditional Congolese food. There was fufu, pondu, and some baked fish called makayabu. I figured right there, that it was as good a time as any for them to witness some real African culture. Lionel joined us at the table and said grace before we went on to serve ourselves. We had to explain to Chris and John what everything was; they too seemed eager to try it actually.

With a fork and knife, they each cut into the fish and took a bite. "Mmm, that's really good," Chris said. "Yeah, it actually reminds me of how my grandma makes her fish," John added. Then, with their forks, they scooped off some pondu from their plates and ate it. "Wow! That's really good!" they exclaimed. I knew that they would love the pondu. It is by far the most popular dish in Congo, similar to the manner of popularity that jollof rice has in Ghana or Nigeria. Hearing them say all of these surprisingly put me at ease. I felt comfortable just being my true self, and so I said "Pass me the fufu."

Like I said, a real Congolese person does not eat this type of meal with any silverware. I grabbed some fufu, used it to scoop up some pondu, and then ate it. Then I cut the makayabu too with my hands and ate it that way. I explained to Chris and John that in many African cultures, doing so was the acceptable way to really enjoy the food. That moment felt liberating; to be in my element, explaining my culture, and for them to receive it well was very freeing.

There was nothing else to be ashamed of.

Nowadays, I strongly urge anyone to try some goat meat or oven-baked fish with some fumbwa and plantains. Maybe try some makayabu with pili pili peppers on top of some rice and madesu. Congo even has its own delicious variation of jollof rice. For dessert, try some Congolese beignets, a.k.a. "mikate" or "puff puff." I can talk about the different dishes and their combinations all day long.

Even then, it can be hard sometimes not to feel guilt when you are from a developing country, yet are enjoying large portions regularly and in the most obese country in the world. In Congo, I could just go outside and vividly see the mass effects of hunger and starvation. Just about every time I rode in the backseat of our car in Congo, we got approached by a mother and her child begging us to spare them some money just so they could eat. I often ask myself at times: "What are we spending money on that is more important than securing human access to food and water?"

I really don't believe hunger should have any place in a modern and global society. We have all the production capacity and needed economic resources in the Western world to provide the planet with sanitized water. This is at the very least. We just don't have the will and worse, get hung up on discussions about political philosophies needed to handle the means of production.

When I hear people talk about all the extreme crime and violence which takes place in a lot of developing countries, I say to them, "Hungry and thirsty people are extremists." Of course they are!

Just look at someone you know whenever they go for too long without eating – they will get HANGRY. The whole world's geo-political landscape would be much easier to cope with if people could have secure access to the essentials of life.

I think everyone should be able to dig into some fufu or any African food with their hands and should fully enjoy it. That includes being able to enjoy Ghanaian Jollof rice... the best Jollof rice there is. Yes, I said it!

4

TAP INTO THOSE GENETICS

ONE THING THAT I learned from growing up in Texas, is that American Football is an unofficial religion in the state. The Dallas Cowboys are kept as the number one team in the National Football League in National Television ratings every single year; regardless of how the team is performing. The University of Texas at Austin also has the country's richest college football program. Local community members are more than happy to pay taxes to build bigger high school stadiums. On Friday nights during the fall, those communities completely revolve around those stadium lights shining brightly on those high school football fields.

In the 7th grade, I decided to try out for a spot in the Indian Springs Middle School football team. I didn't know what any of the positions were nor did I know any of the rules, but my neighbor's dad convinced me to be a Running Back. So I tried out, and made the team as a Running Back and Free Safety although I could not catch to save my life. Everyone assumed that I was some type of great athlete simply because I was one of the few Black kids in town. These stereotypes were in full effect in the sports world. Just a few years before my arrival at Indian Springs, my friend Lionel had just set the school record on the High Jump in track and field games. Here are some of the things I would often hear amongst my teammates:

"Don't Black people have an extra muscle or something in their legs?"

"No, idiot, it's an extra bone in their foot!"

"Of course Yves can jump that high. He knows how to tap into those genetics."

I didn't know what kind of science books from which they got this information, but all of it sounded good to me! My family is not a sports family whatsoever. When we lived in Africa, I remember my sister Patricia giving tennis a try and my brother Lionel trying soccer too. I was a skinny kid who had some shiftiness, some jumping ability, but zero football knowledge or skills. My middle school football coach, Coach Vargas, saw my athletic ability and desperately wanted me to become his Punt Returner and Kickoff Returner. But my hands were so bad that it did not matter. He would make me practice catching punts every single day of practice. That did not help.

My parents valued our education and placed it above any extracurricular activity. I had fun playing sports, but they were very casual for me. I didn't necessarily value them. I remember a time when I was lifting weights in the middle school weight room with some classmates and thought that I could bench press 95 pounds. I put two 25-pound plates on each side of the barbell, laid flat on the bench, lifted the bar off the rack, and it fell straight onto my nose!

The damage would have been horrible if my teammate Matt was not there to quickly grab the weight off of me when he noticed that I could not handle it. I had a lot of fun playing football. In the last game of the season in 8th grade, I scored four rushing touchdowns in the pouring rain and was also named Player of the Game. I received a letter in the mail from Coach Kevin Atkinson, who was the Head Coach of Keller High School. The letter was congratulating me for a great performance and said that he was looking forward to meeting and coaching me. I did not think much of it at the time, but it did feel good to be acknowledged for what I had done on the football field.

My favorite part about football was that I could violently hit people without me getting in trouble for it. By the fall of my 10th grade football season at Keller High School, I weighed about 140 pounds at 5 feet, 7 inches. For some reason, that year, I thought I was bigger than I was and I regularly tried to initiate contact with guys who were bigger than me. It was during an in-game collision when I tried to directly tackle an opposing player, who weighed at least 60 pounds more than me, that I ended up with an unfamiliar pain on my lower back. I played through it and finished the game, but the feeling continued to aggravate me during the following week.

I kept stretching, thinking to myself that it was just a case of sore muscles, but the pain wouldn't go away. I finally told my parents about it and after a visit to the doctor's office, we realized that I had a stress fracture on the 4th vertebrae of my spine. It was the middle of the season and the team was terrible anyway; so it was time for me to start rehabilitating ahead of the following year. During the rehab, all of my attitudes towards football changed. It was November of 2006 and I had to begin a rehab program that went on for eight months. My Physical Therapist gave me a hard, plastic, white shell to wrap around my torso starting from my upper abdominals and going down to my hips.

Wearing that back brace was dreadful. I hated that thing with a passion.

My rehabilitation program consisted of 12 weeks of no athletic activity, followed by another 12 weeks of limited activity (jogging and core exercises), after which there was a possibility that I could start lifting weights again in the final 8 weeks of the rehab. Normally, after football season was over, I would go straight into activities done in the track season. I ran multiple events for the school, but my specialty was the high jump. Again, I lived in Texas; so the way the coaches saw it, track season was good for preparing you for football. Soccer was good for helping your footwork for football season. We had a power-lifting team, which itself was good because it helped you get strong for football. Basketball and baseball were good because activities done in them increased your hand-eye coordination for football. And if you were not playing any of those other sports, you were an essential part of the football strength & conditioning program.

I did not realize how much love I had for football until I could no longer do it. My casual attitude towards sports began to change when I was forced to simply sit back in that awful back brace and watch my teammates train and get bigger, faster, and stronger. By the time February rolled around and the first 12 weeks of inactivity were done, I was super excited to start training again that I did something which I had never done before... I started doing it by myself, without anybody telling me to. That was when I knew that I was truly becoming self-driven. I ran three miles and performed 300 push-ups every single day. I used to pray to God, asking that He would heal my back and lead me to something to help throw that stupid back brace away. I had to wear that thing everywhere – to class, to church, even to the movies. The only time I could take it off, was when I was sleeping, showering, or cleaning it.

My prayers were answered. The doctors cleared me to get rid of the back brace and to start training with my teammates again. I had never been more excited to touch iron weights, and I had a lot of catching up to do. Entering the 11th grade, I played strictly one position: Cornerback. My endurance was high and I still felt fast, but my hips felt a lot stiffer than before. I did not get to have a full offseason like the rest of my team, but I still stuck with the process and played that entire season without any injuries. By the following off season (the one that led up to my senior year), I had never been more devoted to anything else up to that point in my life. There is a country song by Brad Paisley called Anything Like Me. In it, he sings about his firstborn son and with these lyrics: "Won't he be a sight with his football helmet on. That'll be his first love 'til his first love comes along." When I hear that song today, I still feel those lyrics. By that point, I knew I had fallen in love with football.

During the off season, Coach Atkinson called me into his office to inform me that the whole coaching staff was proud of my commitment to the game. Hearing him say that made me never want to let him down. By the time our winter training program was over, I had clocked the fastest 40-yard-dash time on the football team. During spring practices, the coaches often made me take all of the live reps. During summer two-a-days in the scorching heat, I knew I wanted to push myself so hard that my body would hate me by the end of practice. In fact, I even had to go to the emergency room on multiple occasions due to having full body cramps in the Texas heat. I didn't care; I loved football. I wanted to have a great senior season, and then go on to play in college.

What I did not know however, was that it was possible to get a scholarship to play collegiately. Outside of the United States, intercollegiate athletics is an unfamiliar concept. As far as I knew then, I would go to college and just try out for the football team like I had done in high school. If my parents knew at the time, that there was a way for me to get recruited to a university and get all of my college education paid for from me being good at football, you better believe they too would have been more invested in my football skills...and so would I. I did not have any guidance on college recruiting or sending my football tapes to coaches around the country when I was applying for college. I just went out there and played my best game during my last season as a high school football player.

The last game of my high school football career was the biggest emotional roller coaster I have ever experienced. We needed to win in order for us to have a chance at making the playoffs. The game was also against our district rival, Fossil Ridge High School. Keller vs. Fossil was ranked as one of the top high school football rivalries which existed in north Texas at the time. We did not like them and they did not like us. What made that night so great, was that we did not just beat them, but we dominated. It was our first win against them in years and the celebration was on. As the fans were cheering when the clock hit zero, I ran back to the locker room with my teammates, all of us chanting and hooting and hollering!

There was a three-way tie in our district for the final two playoff spots. It was agreed upon before the season began, that if this situation occurred, the two playoff spots would be decided using a coin flip. Keller,

*Yves after the Spring football game during the
offseason before senior year at Keller High*

Colleyville Heritage, and Northwest were the three high schools waiting for a coin flip to decide the fate of their season. As quickly as the celebration began, it ended in an even quicker mood. Keller was the odd team out after the coin flip. The coaches came into our locker room with tears in their eyes to deliver us the bad news. The parents and families joined them shortly after. This thing that the whole community was passionate about came crashing painfully. It was even more devastating for the seniors on the team. Season over. High school playing career done. I got in my car and I cried all the way home.

That following spring, I was invited to participate in the regional track meet happening in Lubbock, TX. I still love track & field even today, same with basketball. But there was something different for me about the sport of football. The camaraderie, the mission, and the sacrifice made it the greatest team game which I had ever known. When I went to Oklahoma State University on an academic scholarship, I tried out for the football team whilst there. I remember Coach Scott Yielding leaving me a voicemail where he informed me that I had made the football team and I remember how I just fell on my knees to pray and thank God.

I do believe that being an athlete sped up the maturity in my personal life. Some transferable skills included that of goal-setting, team building, resiliency, overcoming fear of failure, time management, and the ability to think critically. When I was trying to figure out what career path I wanted to take, I was always inspired by what Nelson Mandela did when he rallied all of South Africa to support their national rugby team during the 1995 Rugby World Cup. Mandela was very strategic in how he galvanized Black and white South Africans alike to root for their country, during a period when racial tensions were so thick in the air that one could cut them with a knife.

I remember thinking to myself, "What else besides sports can unite people in such fashion?"

I wondered how much unification could come out of Congo if the country was able to rally behind their national teams. There are some incredible athletes in Congo who have had to leave the country to play professionally for other nations. How great could it be if people like these had the resources to train at a high level in Congo and went on to be worldwide contenders in sports like soccer, basketball, and rugby? They could also have an opportunity to come to the United States to compete athletically and get their education funded. I believe therefore that it is my duty to provide them with those opportunities.

5

THE RIVER AND THE RESERVOIR

MY FATHER WAS born in Lowa, a city found in the Oriental province on the east side of the Democratic Republic of Congo. In 1921, legend has it, that his grandparents were casted out into that territory because of their close relationship with a famous Congolese prophet named Simon Kimbangu who claimed to heal the sick, prophesy, and revive the dead. Back then, the colony was still very much under Belgian rule. The Belgian religious leaders arrested Kimbangu as his popularity grew and as his ministry spread throughout the region. He was arrested, and this was done along with 11 other people. Among them was my great grandfather, David Batoba, who was also his assistant. He shared handcuffs with Kimbangu himself. All 12 of them got sentenced to life imprisonment in Elisabethville. While they were boating on the Congo River on their way to Elisabethville, they stopped in Lowa and let everyone out. That was except Simon Kimbangu, who continued to a prison in Elisabethville where he was kept for the remaining 30 years of his life.

In Lowa, my great grandfather was made to perform forced labor in an unfamiliar area. Two years later, in 1923, their wives were allowed to join them. Marie Mpolo, my great grandmother, then gave birth to Anne Tusikila, my grandmother.

Even while Simon Kimbangu was in prison, his followers kept growing. The Kimbangu church grew rapidly all along the Congo River. The Belgian leaders were so angered by this, that they arrested 360,000 families and sent them all to live in Loma. In Loma, Andre Matuku met and married Marie Luvemba, who then gave birth to Mathieu Meto.

Mathieu Meto would go on later to marry Anne Tusikila who gave birth to my father in 1956. Named David Batoba, my father was born into a family that did slave work in a region that they were outcasted to by colonizers in Belgian Congo. If you ask my dad today, he'll tell you he was born in prison. As bad as prison is, his family's condition sounds a whole lot worse than prison to me. It was in 1960, that Congo gained its independence from Belgium's government and it was then, that the family was able to relocate to Kinshasa, moving to the Kasa-Vubu neighborhood.

Today, Lowa remains the headquarters of the rebel soldiers who constantly battle with Rwandan troops over mineral resources. It is a warzone. The level of poverty that my dad's family experienced is something I cannot even imagine. Even more, there was no opportunity for any of them there to get a good education until they all moved back to Kinshasa, starting first with my father's generation.

The only hope that my dad had of making it out of generational poverty was to get a good education for himself. His older brother had received the opportunity to go study at one of the best universities in the country, University of Mbandaka, but unfortunately, he fell victim to the carefree lifestyle and neglected his studies in the process. When it was my father's turn to pursue higher education, his parents told him that they would do anything and everything to ensure that he graduated and used that education to provide for the family. It is often said that education is key. For my father, it became the only thing that he could hang his hope on.

Science, Technology, Engineering, Mathematics, and Law.

If you are not studying with the intent of specializing in one of these above-mentioned areas, it is usually seen as a waste of time. When dad enrolled in the University of Kinshasa, he focused on the mathematics realm and soon became a guru in Accounting. It was during my dad's sophomore year of college in 1978 that he met my mom. My mother grew up in the 20-Mai neighborhood, just a 15-minute drive away from where my dad grew up. Even though the neighborhoods were not far in distance, the lifestyles they lived were totally different. 20-Mai was the richer, more established part of Kinshasa. My mother's family was a lot better off compared to my father's family. Despite their different upbringings, they both sparked a friendship that eventually blossomed into a marriage in 1984 which is still going strong.

When I ask my mom to describe what my dad was like in his youth, she usually tells me that he was very charismatic. She says that he always made sure that he was presentable in appearance and took his studies very seriously. Not much has changed even now. I recently asked my dad how he was able to prevent himself from becoming just another product of his environment. His reply was this: "I had to be very good at knowing schoolwork, but I also had to be very good at knowing life." Education is much more than schooling. He was always observant and cognizant of his environment. He ensured that he was book smart and street smart.

Upon graduating from the university, my dad had to take a test in order to work at a publicly owned company called ONATRA; it operates the railways, ports, and river transport in the Congo River. He scored the highest score in all of the test's history. He would later work his way up to becoming the Director of Treasury and eventually he was overseer of all of the company's finances as the Chief Financial Officer. In such a highly-esteemed position, he would then use that to provide jobs within the company for his siblings. This while being the financial support of his entire family.

All of the blood, sweat, tears, and knowledge that went into becoming established in Congo did not mean much when we arrived in the

United States. My parents had to relearn everything. There were many nights that my dad stayed up into the late hours of the night, taking online courses in order for him to graduate with his MBA from the University of Phoenix. Not only was he learning the rules of business, but both of my parents also took community college courses learning how to speak English when they were in their 40's.

The mobility prospects for immigrants in wage and salary employment can often be low. Immigrants' credentials and education from their home country may not be formally recognized in the United States. In addition, when they do not know English very well, they may also experience racial or ethnic discrimination when applying for jobs. That's why it is not uncommon to see immigrants use entrepreneurship instead as a mobility strategy. Oftentimes, immigrants who share an ethnic identity work together to build successful businesses, employing one another and helping each other learn about new business opportunities, many of which will come from within their own co-ethnic communities.

For my parents and indeed for a lot of first generation immigrants, education is the KEY for unlocking opportunities. Grade point average, tests, quizzes, report cards, and IQ scores. The aforementioned are some of the things which my parents emphasized in our 8-person household.

A 2018 report carried out by the Pew Research Center, found that 69 percent of sub-Saharan African immigrants in the United States have had some college education. That number is six percentage points higher than the level for native-born Americans. Thousands of sub-Saharan African immigrants come to the United States through the State Department's diversity visa lottery, which usually provides 50,000 permanent resident visas annually to people from countries that have low rates of immigration to the United States. Two of those lottery winners included my cousin Natacha in 2012 and my cousin Deo in 2008, both of whom stayed with my family as they took advantage of the opportunities here to pursue higher education in America and eventually ended up with Bachelor's degrees and promising career paths.

Despite having high education and employment rates, Black immigrants — including those from Africa, the Caribbean, Central America and South America — have a median household income that's lower than the U.S. average, according to what the Pew researchers found.

To add, 40 percent of Black immigrants are homeowners, 24 percent less than the overall U.S. population, and 20 percent of Black immigrants live below the poverty line, compared to 16 percent of the overall U.S. population.

How can that be? How are so many African immigrants getting advanced degrees and finding employment at a high rate, yet still face challenges to get access to all the opportunities that other groups enjoy? I learned pretty quickly while I was in college, that it wasn't necessarily the smartest people who got the best jobs after graduation. For a long time, I too saw education as a reservoir— it was after all where I went to memorize and regurgitate what the teacher had taught me about facts and figures.

In 1894, the science writer and novelist Grant Allen published the following quote in his book, *Post-Prandial Philosophy*:

One year in Italy with their eyes open would be worth more than three at Oxford; and six months in the fields with a platy scopic [having a wide and flat field of view] lens would teach them strange things about the world around them that all the long terms at Harrow and Winchester have failed to discover to them. But that would involve some trouble for the teacher. **What a misfortune it is that we should thus be compelled to let our boys' schooling interfere with their education!**

The reservoir I used to go to wasn't to get an education. It was schooling me. I realized in college that I wasn't asking myself the insatiable questions that I used to ponder as a child. I realized that I had stopped really thinking for myself. The reservoir did not encourage in me an inquisitive mind, critical thinking, and creativity. Rather, I learned simply to memorize and regurgitate what the teacher taught me. My schooling was about facts and figures, rather than building understanding and creating better moral formation. When I came to this realization, I had to then stop going to the reservoir, and instead, I went to the river of education. The river is one which bends, yields, bounds, and splashes against rocks. Most importantly, the river continually flows. Education is something that must become a way of life.

When I arrived on my university's campus, the value of an education had been embedded in me. I was taught prior to that, that if I got a great education, it would lead afterwards to a great job upon graduation. My plan initially was to study Sports Media and then go on to become an on-air radio or television host. After my freshman year of college, I had a change of heart and a growing passion for the business of sports, which led to a switch in my major to Business Administration, Sports Management, and adding Marketing later on. I remember a classmate of mine who didn't take his grades as seriously as I did. "C's get degrees," was what he would always say. His focus was ensuring that he did enough to meet the bare minimum in order to pass and graduate. To my surprise, after he graduated, he became a Vice President at a prestigious private jet company! The guy who barely made it to graduation landed a job like this?! HOW?

So I went flowing in the river and I researched the company that this classmate of mine went to work at. I read their mission statement, company history, and took a look at their staff. It was there in that staff section that I discovered that his best friend was also hired as a VP in the same company. Well, the best friend himself was the grandson of the company's founder.

Now it all made sense.

This classmate of mine was associated with the right person. His friend was a product of nepotism and because they were both connected, he hired him within the company and quickly elevated him. So I remember venting about this to an Academic Advisor at my university during a casual conversation. She told me something that changed the way I approached the rest of my college career. "Yves, I know that you know how important education is. But remember this," she continued and said.... "You are either in the people business or you're out of business."

You are either in the people business or you're out of business.

This phrase above changed everything for me. For all I know, the guy who became a Vice President may not have been great in school, but maybe he was equipped on the inner workings of that specific company. I have no idea. What I do know is that I truly believe that any immigrant that comes to the United States has to get outside of their comfort zone to cultivate genuine friendships with the individuals around them, especially when they are on a college campus. These friendships often lead to conversations about topics one wouldn't consider, which then leads to curiosity, which leads to reading books about that topic and eventually self-educating. Every job I have had along my career path since graduating college came as a result of somebody referring me for the said job.

I often say that the greatest education I received in college didn't come from what the professors taught me, but rather from the intentional conversations I had with staff and other students. For example, my friend Justin – a white guy who has lived in Oklahoma his entire life – challenged how I interpreted biblical scripture, he pushed me to operate with integrity, and we grew a friendship so close that I was the best man at his wedding. I also had an atheist friend who, although she didn't believe in Jesus, understood how to extend grace to people and that was also something that rubbed off on me.

The most influential peer I met in college however was my best friend Elliott. Elliott and I became roommates during my sophomore year, which was his freshman year. He was from a small town called Batesburg-Leesville in the middle of South Carolina and was one of the most unique people I've ever met. He was a Black man with a strong Southern country accent who loved hunting, fishing, and farming. He was one of the best high school football players in his state and he also won a state championship in soccer. One second, he could be blasting rap music and the next, he was singing country songs at the top of his lungs. On the outside, Elliott didn't appear to ever take himself too seriously. He was just as easy going as I was and we easily got along from the moment we first met. The first time we went to a college party, he couldn't believe how people of different races were co-mingling. He asked me, "Ay boe, you sure good to be in here? We can just talk to these white girls publicly like this?"

It was a brand new experience for him. Mind you, that was happening in the year 2010! When we went back to the apartment after that first party, he couldn't wait to call his hometown friends to tell them what had just happened. "I gotta call the homies. They ain't gon' believe this!"

The grooms party at Yves' wedding included college friends Elliott, Justin, Christian. Lionel, Nathan, and Trey (brother-in-law) were also in the wedding.

Elliott would often tell me stories about having guns pointed at him back in South Carolina because his conversations with the white girls at his high school were a little too friendly. I remember listening to him often complain about the coded laws and unwritten rules which existed in his home state to ensure that his family, and other Black people, did not gain too much power. "They run our town like a plantation!" He would tell me, "My mama had to make sure that she didn't sound too intelligent when talking to my teachers and coaches just so they wouldn't purposely try to hold us back...I could have stayed to play college ball in the state, but I had to get the hell up outta there!"

Elliott's family is Gullah Geechee. They are a population of the United States that don't get talked about enough, in my opinion. The Gullah Geechee are a group of people who live on the coastal plains and Sea Islands of South Carolina from Jacksonville, NC to Jacksonville, FL. After being brought to America through the Port of Charleston, they eventually outnumbered the whites living in the Sea Islands and coast. They refused to assimilate, and so they created their own creole language, food, and way of life that is rich and draws heavily from their original West African culture. It is my friendship with Elliott that sparked the curiosity in me to go and learn about the Black history that I wasn't taught in school. Elliott would say to me "Being Black is not just the skin tone but the combination of the biology, experience, and psychology."

He continued by saying, "Biology matters first because Black folks are not a monolith, but are viewed as such through the lenses of current social construct on a global scale. People would be surprised to learn that the genetic diversity present in Africa is greater than any other region in the world. Experience, because there has to be an understanding of your ethnic identity. If you leave it up to the history books and the mainstream media, you'd think Black people were barbaric and ignorant animals before being brought over to the United States. When you look at the actual history beyond the textbooks, you realize that we had structured, civilized systems that were foundational in the development of the world as we know it. Finally, psychology because there is an enormous amount of unlearning and relearning that has to be done. This brings the analogy of the river vs. the reservoir."

It has to be done by you first knowing yourself and learning about where you came from. Go see a therapist if you must! Or you can talk to the elders in your family. It was through intentional questions with my parents that I recently learned that my family comes from the Bakongo tribe, with my mother's side being from the Mboma clan and my father coming from the Musingobe clan.

As they often say in the Gullah Geechee culture, "Hunnuh mus tek cyare de root fa heal de tree."

Simply put: When the roots are deep, there is no reason to fear the wind.

In February of 2012, Elliott and I attended a Black History Month event held on campus to support one of our friends who was singing on stage that day. What we didn't know was that we would walk out with a crucial lesson about American Black history that neither one of us had ever heard of. One of the speakers at the event was a survivor of the Black Wall Street Massacre which took place about an hour away from our college campus in 1921. He told the audience about how he was a boy growing up in a thriving community on the North side of Tulsa, OK. The community didn't need anything from anyone outside of it. It was made up of the following:

- 600 businesses
- 21 restaurants
- 21 churches
- A school system
- A bus system
- Multiple law offices
- 30 grocery stores

- 2 movie theaters
- 6 private planes
- 1 Post Office
- 1 hospital
- 1 bank

They called it the Black Wall Street, a place that was the wealthiest Black community in the United States. He told us about the day when nearby white residents came into their community and proceeded to burn and destroy more than 35 square blocks of the district, and then created the new fire code laws to ensure that the community would not be able to rebuild. This massacre left 10,000 black people homeless.

We couldn't believe that neither of us had ever heard about this before then. Whenever I would bring it up to people who spent their entire lives in Oklahoma, even they too said they were unaware of the Black Wall Street massacre. Why wouldn't they teach about this massive part of history in schools? Again: The river vs. the reservoir.

6 | GOOD INTERNET FOR YOUR SOUL

I HAD A neighbor in Congo who used to practice witchcraft and sorcery. I remember a time when my sister Laetitia and I climbed on top of our front gate to look over the fence into the neighbor's courtyard and we saw her doing all sorts of dancing and rituals almost like she was calling upon spirits. My mom came out from inside the house and yelled at us to get down. She would explain to us later, "There are spirits that come from God and other spirits that come from the devil. You have to know what to guard yourself from." At a very young age, it was not uncommon for me to start learning about the supernatural.

Topics about witchcraft and sorcery were not out of the ordinary to learn about. People would often share stories about people they knew being possessed by evil spirits, or even seeing a pastor cast demons out of someone. I remember being 6 years old and seeing a lady screaming at the top of her lungs and then falling to the ground when she heard the name Jesus. When we were living in South Africa, I overheard some pastors reading about the Apocalypse towards the end of the Bible and I remember wanting to have absolutely nothing to do with that book. It just sounded way too scary for me.

After arriving at our apartment in Irving, TX in the late 90's we were immediately plugged into the Congolese community in the Dallas/ Fort Worth metroplex. There is a joke that if you are a Congolese person in Dallas/Fort Worth, you know EVERYONE in the area who is Congolese. I assumed that every one of them were born in Congo and moved to the U.S...

It wasn't until decades later that I found out some of them were born in the USA and were considered as second-generation immigrants. Young, old, rich, poor, first-generation immigrant, second-generation immigrant, we knew them all and we leaned on each other as we assimilated to American life. The boys for instance, would often recap what happened in the latest episode of WWF wrestling and then try to imitate the moves when the adults were not around.

I went to school with some of them, where we attended English as a Second Language (ESL) programs together, along with other immigrants and international boys and girls who came from China, India, Sudan, and different parts of Africa. I took these classes in the 2nd, 3rd, and beginning of 4th grade. Halfway through 4th grade, we left Irving and moved into the suburb of Keller, TX where they did not offer the program due to a lack of an international presence in the town. I however didn't need it anymore as I had become fluent in English at 9 years old.

The church that my family attended, Mountain of Prayers, was a Christian church with a mostly Congolese congregation and felt very in tune with the Holy Spirit. It was very reminiscent of attending church in Kinshasa, just minus the translator on stage for those who were not as fluent in French or Lingala which is a Bantu language spoken throughout the northwestern part of the Democratic Republic of Congo and a large part of the Republic of Congo. Growing up as a kid in church, I did not really question much about faith. I knew that I believed in God and tried to ask for forgiveness any time I did anything sinful. That was about the extent to which my spiritual life went.

Celebrating a birthday with members of the
Congolese community from church

When I began college, I had two teammates both named Andrew, who inspired me by the way that they lived their lives as devoted Christians. Observing how they lived their lives every day provided me a real example of what masculine Christianity looked like amongst my peers. I had seen older men live out their faith, but not too many in my age group. The summer before my sophomore year in college, I was having a conversation in the kitchen with one of the Andrews about Jesus Christ. Although I was aware that the Father, Son, and Holy Spirit made up the Holy Trinity I did not have a good understanding of the Gospel. During my conversation with Andrew, he challenged me to read one chapter from the book of John in the bible every day, and every day we would have a discussion. I accepted his challenge.

On the third day, while we were discussing chapter 3 of John, Andrew attempted to explain the Gospel of Jesus Christ to me. He took out a piece of paper, turned it horizontally, and drew two stick figures on the far left. "This is me and you," said Andrew. On the far right, he drew a big circle with a capital "G" in it, saying "This is God. Let's say that all of this space in between us and God is the Grand Canyon. It is impossible for us to walk across and get to where God is. Even this drawing is a very poor illustration of how far we are from Him. He is perfect and we are messy and full of sin!" Andrew then proceeded to draw a bridge that stretched from us to God and said, "That's the cross." He then went on to explain that God came over to where we were standing, became a man, took on our sin, and the cross bridged the gap between us and God. "The Father is God. Jesus in God as a human. The Holy Spirit is also God and helps us on this bridge."

That was the clearest explanation of the Gospel that I had ever heard up to that point in my life. Three months later, in October of 2010, I made the conscious decision to fully commit my life to Christ, and it was then that I really began to question faith and seek answers. At some point, my understanding of Jesus and salvation moved from "This is just what we do at church. We whoop and holler about the Lord," to "I now have a desire to learn about the things of God."

I started reading more books and also I started attending different church communities. I went from the African church, to the African American church, and even to the white evangelical church. One of the main questions I had when I was in college came when I started attending a church with a largely white population (which also happens to be the dominant, broader church experience in America).

"Why does this feel different?" I would ask myself.
"It feels more......academic."

I was hearing different Biblical commentaries, lexicons, and learning about church history. This was all stuff which I had never heard before! It was exciting because I was accustomed to getting a piece of scripture, talking about it for 45 minutes, and then spending another couple of hours singing about it. But even though I was enticed by this type of church experience, I still felt a conflict arise within me.

I would then remember the different levels of spirituality that I grew up witnessing. People using their spiritual gifts, church members speaking in tongues out loud, worship that would last forever because the weight of the Holy Spirit was felt in the church building. It felt like the white church understood the bible, but the church experience I grew up in however was one that understood the struggles of the world. It felt like I may have been getting a better intellectual understanding of things that were divine while there, but I wasn't getting the same type of holy spirit encounters that I got when I'd go back home and we'd have family prayers or even when I visited the typical American Black church.

So I started to research more in hopes of finding an answer to my question: "Why does this feel so different?" There were infinite amounts of writings about the Gospel, the Puritans, and the 16th century Church of England. The whole time I was reading up on all these things, in the back of my mind I had these thoughts:

"Why didn't they stop slavery then?"

"Didn't some of these dudes own slaves?"
"Not a single one of them said anything about the mistreatment of Black people?!"

I didn't know. My faith started to feel contrary to the things I valued, leading me to an identity crisis and a deep desire to want to connect more to my original African identity. Because of God, I knew we were able to make it out of the war with our full health. I knew that as soon as I graduated from college, I had to take a trip back to the mother-land and try to reconnect SOMEHOW. Towards the end of 2013, I went on a life-changing trip to Kenya (more about this trip in a later chapter). There was a man I met in Kenya who said something to me that I thought was very profound.

He said, "It is so easy to lose yourself in Western countries like America, because it doesn't take much to get distracted."

People walk with their eyes on their phones, erotic images are a part of everyday life, and the instant you feel bored, you get on social media. Does society place an importance on prayer? Does the culture value your soul? Not to mention, the richer you get, the more intentional and deliberate you have to be, because it is easier to access distractions.

The man said too "The devil has to work hard here in Africa. He has to work hard in Trinidad and Tobago, and in India. In America, the devil only needs to give you good internet for your soul."

After graduating college, I started noticing that something great was happening in America. There seemed to be a reemergence of people embracing African cultures. Black Americans had a desire to connect with their original African heritage. Back in the late 90's and early 2000's, it was not cool to be African whatsoever. Growing up as the only African kid in most of my social circles, I used to hear a lot of cruel jokes. "African booty scratcher" is something that I heard often from the Americans. It did not help that the news and the National

Geographic documentaries over-represented the worst parts of the African continent.

By the time the 'Black Panther' movie came out in theaters and Beyoncé's musical film/visual album 'Black is King' too, you could see that artists were emphasizing African roots. One thing that I would caution however, is that it is important to have the distinction to not glorify wickedness and then call that Black culture. In Ephesians 6:12, the Apostle Paul says "Our struggle is not against flesh & blood but against principalities & powers, the rulers of the darkness of this world, & spiritual wickedness in high places." And yes, sometimes that darkness comes packaged as great visuals and cinematography and that can cause us to stumble. The blatant glorification of ancestral spirits in the name of Black culture can completely contradict what I believe. I had to remember to guard my soul always. This was especially true when dealing with matters of westernized religion.

7

JESUS OF NAZARETH, TEXAS

IT IS ONE thing to be patriotic and it is a whole different thing to be someone from Texas. It is quite possible that the majority of Texans love the state of Texas more than they do the United States of America. In elementary and middle school, we learned about U.S. history and then we had a separate curriculum strictly focused on Texas history. Every morning when school began, all students were to recite the pledge of allegiance to the flag of the United States of America and that was immediately followed with a pledge to the Texas flag.

"Honor the Texas flag; I pledge allegiance to thee, Texas, one and indivisible."

This was followed by a moment of silence, as required by Texas law. After going away to college one state away, I would later say to myself, "If I didn't grow up in Texas, I don't know if I would like Texans." The amount of pride felt was arrogant, but even though I recognized it, it existed in me too. DON'T MESS WITH TEXAS. Although there are dozens of stereotypes that exist about people who are from the Lone Star State, I can confirm that these few are true for the majority of folks living in the state: Football is sacred, the state will vote Republican in almost any election, and they believe in the Bible.

There is a region in the Southern part of the United States referred to as "The Bible Belt" in which religious beliefs there play a strong role in society and politics. Church attendance is higher in the Bible belt than the national average and the majority of people consider religion to be a very important part of their lives. My family fit right into the Bible Belt, as we came into the country already having our Christian faith. I for one used to attend a local youth ministry near Fort Worth on Wednesdays with a friend from school. The preaching there was pretty forgettable, but I mostly went because they had games to play and because there were cute girls there to talk to from different schools. This youth ministry was very different from the church that I attended with my parents on Sundays. Church on Sundays for me was a lot more buttoned up. We dressed up more formally and the pastor preached with even more enthusiasm and zeal. I did not think much about the contrast of the churches, other than "Black churches operate one way and white churches operate another way."

There was a time I was at the barbershop when a conversation broke out about the skin color of Jesus. I was about 16 years old at the time and I had never given much thought to what race the messiah was. One of the guys waiting on his haircut started going on a tangent about the church and its role in politics and in the brainwashing of individuals. He continued to say controversial statements which I had never really questioned about my religion before. Statements such as:

- "Why should I believe that a white man saved my soul?"
- "Didn't the slave masters use the very same Bible to keep us in bondage?"
- "Are you really going to let the oppressor have control of your spirituality?"
- "Don't you know his name wasn't even Jesus?"
- "You know he was an immigrant, right? Someone might want to tell the voters that Jesus is from Nazareth in Israel and not Nazareth, TX!" (That's a real city)

I went to the barbershop for a haircut but I left with a puzzled head. This random stranger had me questioning everything I knew about my faith. I was having a hard time reconciling Christianity with my original ethnic identity. This idea that Christianity is the white man's religion is one which has become a major stumbling block for many people of African descent. For many Black believers in general, the balancing act of holding onto the faith while staying true to their ethnic heritage is like having a pebble in their shoe. It presents one with a nagging concern that remains in them even as they walk with God. I did what any rational person would do in this situation: I went to the internet for answers.

I did not realize that there were so many blog forums, websites, and webcam pseudo-scholars trying to debunk Christianity.

Was Christianity really intended to benefit white people? What I came to eventually find out later was that nothing could be further from the truth. Christianity doesn't belong to any one race. One of the greatest losses which African Americans suffered during the trans-Atlantic slave trade was a knowledge of their history. They were led to believe for hundreds of years that they had no history worth remembering; in fact, many Black folks also lost the desire to know anything about their African past. They are led to believe that they were brought here on a boat and that everything before that is barbaric!

After going down the rabbit hole of the cyber universe, I decided to go to the Keller Public Library to find more answers. In the book *African Religions and Philosophy*, scholar John S. Mbiti wrote, "Christianity in Africa is so old that it can rightly be described as an indigenous, traditional and African religion." I learned that Africans themselves played such a significant role in early Christianity that the renowned scholar Thomas C. Oden, who holds a Ph.D. from Yale, wrote the following in his book *How Africa Shaped the Christian Mind: Rediscovering the African Seedbed of Christianity*: "Decisive intellectual achievements of Christianity were explored and understood first in Africa before they were recognized in Europe and a millennium before they found their way to North America."

I picked up the book *Biblical Strategies for a Community in Crisis,* which had some great cross-references to the Bible. Someone once told me, that the 3 most important factors to understanding the Bible are:
1) Context
2) Context
3) Context!

In this book, it explains that the Bible corrects any deception of racial prejudice. The Bible mentions historically Black nations like Ethiopia, Cush, Canaan and Egypt more than 1,000 times. Conversely, the European nations like Rome (20) and Greece (30) are mentioned just 50 times combined. Not to mention that 1600 years before the transatlantic slave trade, Acts 2:41 tells us that Peter preached the gospel in an African nation. Surely, out of the 3,000 men who received Christ that day, some of them (if not most of them) must have been Black men.

In Acts 8:26-39, we read about an "Ethiopian eunuch of great authority" who accepted Christ after he heard the gospel from the Apostle Philip. In Biblical times, the word Ethiopia did not just describe the country which is known by that name today. Instead, it referred to all of Africa which was south of Egypt. Well in verse 37, the Ethiopian says, "I believe that Jesus Christ is the Son of God." So again, 1600 years before the African Slave Trade began, Black men were giving their lives to Jesus Christ and becoming Christians. In Acts 11, we read about an interesting episode in which Africans served as missionaries to Europeans.

Centuries before Europeans entered West Africa and the Congo to be missionaries, African men were taking the gospel to people in Greece. Or in Acts 13, where we see that two of the three men who laid hands on the Apostle Paul and sent him out to spread the gospel were Africans. One of them was Lucius of Cyrene (Cyrene was a thriving Black Christian community in Libya), and the other one was a man whose name was Simon called Niger, which literally translates to "The Black Man." They prayed and fasted with Paul and Barnabas before they sent them out on their missionary journey.

I was infatuated with all of this new-found knowledge. I even called Malek to tell him that Africa's Nubian kingdom, which included what is now known as Sudan, was once a Christian nation without being subject to Roman rule.

In the city of Dallas alone, there were men like Dr. Tony Evans and Bishop T.D. Jakes who graced the pulpits there every single week. Black men who were excellent communicators and are well-versed in teaching the Bible. I thought to myself, "Surely they are educated enough to know that they are not teaching about a religion meant to keep them oppressed."

One of the greatest quotes that I came across in all of my readings and research was by Marcus Garvey, the Jamaican activist/publisher/entrepreneur. He said, "I believe in God the Father, God the Son, and God the Holy Spirit. I believe that Jesus died and rose for me. I believe that God lives for me as for all men, and no condition you can impose upon me by deceiving me about Christianity will cause me to doubt Jesus Christ and to doubt God. I shall never hold Christ responsible for the commercialization of Christianity by the heartless men who adopt it as the easiest means of fooling and robbing other people out of their land and country."

That commercialization is one that is especially evident in the Bible Belt. It is said that the USA is a country which was founded on Christian principles. "In God We Trust" is printed on the dollar bill and the Ten Commandments are also written out in the Supreme Court Buildings. Then, I think about how Native Americans and Africans were treated poorly from the very beginning; essentially going against those commandments. It was Dr. Martin Luther King, Jr. who said that "at 11 o'clock on Sunday morning is one of the most segregated hours, if not the most segregated hour, in Christian America." The eyes through which most people view Christianity is shaped by their own cultural experience. Unfortunately, because of the segregation within the church, most people don't care enough to gain a different perspective.

One perspective I was interested in learning about as I entered my 20's was about Jesus and race. What race was Jesus and did it even matter? When I looked at depictions of the Buddha or the different deities from Hinduism, or even Muhammad the prophet and founder of Islam, I noticed that none of them were ever portrayed to be white, even in the United States. But Jesus from Nazareth, TX seemed to be everywhere! The myth of a white Jesus is one that has deep roots throughout Christian history. As early as the Middle Ages and particularly during the Renaissance, popular Western artists depicted Jesus as a white man, one that often had blue eyes and light-colored hair.

I started having these conversations with people who I was close to. A lot of them felt that it did not matter what Jesus looked like, and although I do agree that he is bigger than any race, I could not help asking "Well if it didn't matter then why do we hardly ever see the original paintings and pictures of Jesus and even his disciples?" Furthermore, "Was it because colonizers were trying to subjugate a group of people and turn them into slaves, physically and mentally?"

Jomo Kenyatta, the first Prime Minister and President of Kenya said "When the Missionaries arrived, the Africans had the land and the Missionaries had the Bible. They taught us how to pray with our eyes closed. When we opened them, they had the land and we had the Bible."

There are many existing theories that try to explain Jesus and race. As a person who greatly values unity, I get concerned sometimes that evangelicalism has lost its way. Having attended numerous churches in Texas, I feel confident in saying that the white church has become idolatrous and concerned with being Republican and the Black church has become idolatrous with cultural identity. Idolatry tends to reject the true God in favor of something or of someone else.

On one side, too many people have wrapped their faith in the American and Texan flag. A nationalistic faith has therefore contaminated the Gospel. Not because it is associated with a specific political party, but because it has adjusted to national policies instead of it upholding biblical values relating to social justice. On the other side, a faith that identifies more with being Black than Biblical prioritizes color above Christ. That leads to supporting candidates and policies who endorse things that do not align with the Bible all because of racial issues. God does not ride on the back of either Democrats or Republicans. The unity of the church is a Gospel issue; one that trumps any political differences. I try to stay encouraged through asking questions and seeking the truth using intentional prayer, deliberate research, and real relationship with God.

"Then you will know the truth, and the truth shall set you free." John 8:32.

8 | THE COLOR IS DEEP

I WAS IN the locker room getting ready for practice and there was a conversation taking place among four of my teammates nearby. I wasn't paying any attention to their conversation, as I was focused on putting my gear on. Suddenly, I heard one of them say, "They tried to send a nigger over there to fight me…" I looked up with an angry look on my face and made eye contact with the guy who had said so. The other three noticed that I heard what he said. Right when I stood up to say something, the guy who said it cut me off and said "Calm down. Slavery was like a thousand years ago and you have your freedom. So before you start preaching about that Black power bullshit, I'm not over here being racist."

At that moment, all I wanted was to grab my football helmet and crack his head open with it. I wanted to give him an accurate timeline of slavery. I wanted to educate him on the effects of Jim Crow, segregation, and the lasting psychological effects of being in bondage. I wanted to tell him that no one who was in my family was even enslaved in America! All this while beating his face in. But it was my senior year of football and I couldn't afford to get into any type of trouble and further jeopardize my season. This is just one of the examples of the many frustrations which I felt while coming up.

When you're a Black immigrant, you suffer from double discrimination. Discrimination because you're Black, but in addition, if you have an African accent, institutions stereotype you as being less qualified and also less intelligent. If you speak proper English and get good grades at school, the kids around might call you an "oreo." One who was white on the inside, but Black on the outside. I was never called it, but I heard other Black students referred to as that. All of this despite the data that shows that African immigrants have some of the best grades, some of the highest test scores, and are disproportionately among the most educated people in the United States. Stereotypes simply don't care about facts.

I still remember the very first white person I ever saw. I must have been 5 years old in Congo when I was out on the town with my mom and there was a white gentleman who looked to be in his late 20's or early 30's. I remember this man clearly because he was missing an ear. I don't know if it was a birth defect or something else, but I said to my mom "What's wrong with him? His skin is very light and he only has one ear." I thought that maybe, there was a correlation between being white and losing body organs. "No, some people are just white," my mom said. "They're just like us, just that they are with different color of skin." I still believe that today. Even after all the racist encounters I've had and have witnessed over the years, I still believe that.

When AOL Instant Messenger (AIM) became popular as the best instant-messaging software which was free to download, every grade school kid seemingly was on there, chatting with their friends at all hours of the day, individually and in chat rooms too. One night, while in the 7th grade, I logged on to AIM and I got invited to join a chatroom from a username which I had never seen before. This wasn't uncommon, as new users from school joined in all the time. I accepted the invitation and immediately someone wrote the word "Nigger" upon me entering the chat. Then they wrote it again. Then someone else wrote it. "Go pick some cotton" came from another user. I left the chat. Seconds later, I received another invitation into the same chatroom and I reluctantly accepted it again. The same thing proceeded to happen. I typed in the chat, "Omg what's happening in here??????"

"OMG?!? LOL THAT'S REALLY BLACK."
"Black people use omg???"
"Monkeys these days."

One of the people in the chat messaged me separately and started apologizing profusely. "I'm so sorry! I'm SO sorry! They're such jerks! They are stupid boys that go to Hillwood Middle School. They're so dumb!" So I messaged one of the boys in question separately and told him to meet me at the Hillwood Middle School track on Saturday at 1:00 PM. "I'll make sure you find me," he replied. On Saturday, I grabbed a thick tree branch about as long as a baseball bat and I rode my bike to the Hillwood track. I was fully prepared to fight him that day and anybody else he would have brought along with him. I was furious over the span of two days. It is probably a good thing that nobody eventually showed up that day because it could have turned out horribly for everyone involved.

Those early days of social media with websites like AIM, Xanga, and Myspace were the cause of the majority of fights which I got into. And it usually involved the n-word. There is something about hearing that word, with the aggressive "r" at the end that just draws an instant emotional reaction for most Black folks. Even the spelling of the name looks aggressive. Those two g's which are in the middle look like they're flexing at you. I HATE it. Whenever someone would say it online, I would wait until the next time I saw them and confront them in person. Usually people were a lot braver behind the screen than they often were in person. Even in person, they were not as brave. During one track practice, my friend Ricky was running around the track.

Although Ricky was Mexican, at times he was a bit racially ambiguous – you couldn't really tell what race he was. Well, there was a red-haired white kid nearby watching Ricky run and this kid referred to Ricky as a "sand nigger." When he saw that I heard him, he said "Oh no, I wasn't talking about you, I said the word 'sand' in front of it." I ran up to him, punched him across the face and then proceeded to run. In middle school, I would always make sure that no adults were watching whenever I got in a fight. I can't say the same for my siblings. There was a time when my little brother, Nathan, was in middle school and was suspended for one day for fighting. My parents were furious! When Nathan told them that he fought because the kid called him a racial slur, that anger vanished. I never got caught, but even if I did, I felt it would be justified. I saw it as righteous anger.

I even stopped caring if adults/teachers were present after the 10th grade as a result of an interaction I had with a school administrator. During a passing period, in between classes, my friend Jermaine came up to me and said, "Go to the bathroom and open the door to the third stall. I ain't saying nothing else." What a weird thing to say, but okay. I walked over to the boy's bathroom, where a kid was washing his hands and was headed out. I went over to the third stall and, written in sharp large letters, were the words:

"THE ONLY GOOD NIGGER IS A DEAD NIGGER"

Just underneath the words, was a picture of a noose. I left the bathroom and went to go find Jermaine. "I already told the Principal," he said. "I'm going to go do the same thing," I responded. When I went to the Principal's office, his secretary told me that he was busy, and so I told her to please relay the message over to him. During the following passing period, I was called into the Assistant Principal's office. He took a seat in front of me and asked me to sit down as well. With an earnest look on his face he said, "I heard what you said about the boy's bathroom. That's something we take very seriously. Well, we went in there and looked and there was nothing in the stall."

I asked him, "Are you sure you looked in the right stall? Because more than one person saw it."

"We went in there and there was nothing on the stall."

So I left his office and then went straight to the bathroom, only to find a blank, brand new stall door. The previous one had obviously been replaced somehow. That's when I knew that the replacement was an attempt to avoid a potential PR disaster. It was more important for the school to save face than to even attempt being honest and address the real problem. That happened in the 10th grade, and it was the last time I cared whether or not a school administrator caught me standing up to someone about something racially demeaning.

The following year, I would turn 16 years old and I was looking forward to finally getting my driver's license. My parents were also looking forward to it because I would then be able to drive my younger siblings around to their different events, outings, and obligations. The very first week that I had my driver's license, my dad gave me the permission to take his 2004 Chevrolet Avalanche truck for a quick cruise. So I drove around town to visit 2 or 3 friends to show off my license. On my way back home, I saw a cop car make a turn into the street that I was on and started driving right behind me. After a few seconds, the blue and red lights came on. My heart dropped right away. I pulled into a nearby neighborhood and then turned the car off, waiting for the officer to approach the vehicle. The interaction went something like this:

Cop: "Nice truck! Where are you headed?"
Me: "I'm on my way home from a friend's house."
Cop: "Let me see your license and insurance."

I gave the officer what he requested. After a few minutes, he came back and told me that I was free to go.

Me: "Can you tell me why I got pulled over, sir?"
Cop: "...Get home safe."

No reason. I knew that he legally didn't have to tell me why he pulled me over, therefore I didn't think much of it, other than that, I wish he would have told me what I did wrong so that I could avoid it next time. As I've gotten older and reflected on that day, I realize that I was a Black boy in a great Texas community, driving a nice truck who got pulled over without receiving a reason. I wonder if I was racially profiled. I cannot imagine that a cop in a city with approximately 2% Black people was accustomed to seeing a young person of color driving an expensive truck without raising suspicion. I'll never know why he pulled me over, but what I do know, is I cannot let that thought consume me.

That same year, I had a girlfriend who was Puerto Rican. About 8 months into our year-long relationship, we were talking on the phone and she was tearful because her grandmother had just told her that she would go to HELL because she was dating a Black guy. Now, I had heard some colorful things about my race before, but it was never to that level. Someone was doomed to eternal damnation by association with me! I couldn't even be mad upon hearing this. I just accepted what I once heard my father say: *"There will be people my entire life who simply think less of me because of pure ignorance and stupidity."* That's why when I got to college and a Native American girl I was dating told me that her father told her if she ever brought home a black baby, he would disown her, I wasn't shocked, despite seeing her uncontrollable tears. Sadly, it is just a part of reality.

Some relationships will not materialize because of the large amount of prejudice. I understand how people can let these situations seep into their mindset. By the time I was 18, I had become almost numb to it. Between the hatred we faced as a family in South Africa and what I experienced in the United States, I had built up emotional callouses. Even in adulthood, there were times when my friends and I would get denied access to an establishment because of a "dress code violation," despite us wearing similar clothing as our Caucasian counterparts, we all knew that the dress codes were used to covertly discriminate against us.

I used to naively give people the benefit of the doubt. When an establishment had a sign openly saying they did not want people wearing baggy jeans, sports affiliated jerseys, backwards hats, white tee shirts, or excessive jewelry, I figured it was their prerogative to want people dressed a certain way in their club or restaurant. My thoughts changed one night in downtown Fort Worth when a bar owner asked me and my friend Justin to leave because our pants were too baggy.

We were seated there with three other non-Black friends who were wearing pants that fit them the exact same way. When we went outside and looked at the people that they were letting in, they had on pants that were way baggier than ours. I understood immediately what was going on. They just had those "dress codes" created so that they wouldn't be in violation of any federal discrimination law. After a few episodes like that over the years, I just stopped trying to go to places where I wasn't wanted.

What I can never become numb to, however, is RACISM. It is easy for one to mistake prejudice and discrimination for racism, and I too did not have an understanding of the difference between these things until I was in college. Racism involves people in power preventing another race of people from advancing in life, whether doing so through employment, housing, healthcare, education, criminal justice, and other necessities of life.

I was furious when I learned about the Homestead Act in 1862, which gave 270 million acres of land in the south and west of the Mississippi River to 1.6 million white families and virtually for free. I'm not furious because white people got it, but rather because it is estimated that 46 million white people even today are benefitting from the Homestead Act financially. That's more than the entire population of African Americans today.

Again, The Social Security Act in 1935 was not extended to domestic workers or farmers. It just so happens that then, most African Americans were either domestic workers or farmers. That same year, the Wagner Act created Unions but excluded Black people from having access to union benefits. The G.I. Bill after World War II gave most of its white soldiers benefits such as access to free education and low interest home mortgages; this while most of the 2 million African Americans who fought in World War II were denied those same benefits. The Federal Housing Administration loans from 1934-1962 is another example. It provided 120 billion dollars of government-backed low interest mortgage loans to homeowners. 98% of the people who received these loans were white Americans.

I often wondered, "What is it about darker colored skin that can drive people to such horrific measures?" Even in African nations, colorism is still very real. There are people who buy lightening creams and apply it all over their skin in order to appear lighter. Amongst my African friends and family, I have heard statements like "I can't be in that sun today. I'll get darker." A friend of mine once told me he prefers to call himself brown instead of black because the color black is often associated with negativity, such as evil, darkness, and despair. When I think of the color black, I think of oil, which is the world's most important source of energy. I think of the coal which forms beautiful diamonds and the midnight sky that carries with it unimaginable depth. That's what I think about. The color is deep. Anybody who remains prejudiced or racist shows just how little depth they come with.

9

AMERICAN DREAM REMIXED

IN 2012, I noticed that people were getting bolder with their outspoken hatred, especially online. It started off earlier that year as I was in the second semester of my third year of college. News came out about how a teenage boy named Trayvon Martin was shot and killed in Sanford, FL.

George Zimmerman, a neighborhood watch volunteer, told a 911 dispatcher that there was a "suspicious guy" who was wearing a dark hoodie. Shortly after, Zimmerman fatally shot an unarmed Trayvon Martin, and what ensued, was the beginning of a new wave of conversations on race in America. News stations were having debates about Black people being viewed as threats. Scholars were speaking about implicit biases held at major conferences. Protesters were publicly wearing hoodies over their heads as a symbol of solidarity with the family of Trayvon Martin's. All of the coverage weighed heavily on me. I went on my personal twitter account and I posted a photo of me with a gray hoodie covering my head, with the caption "Will I be next?" I thought to myself that it was an innocent, sincere post.

I couldn't believe the response to that picture.

People came out of nowhere and tried to educate me about how Trayvon Martin was in the wrong. PASSIONATELY defending George

Zimmerman's right to kill a teenage Black boy. Friends and strangers alike. The worst part about it all, as I saw it, was that the narrative seemed like an "Us against them" situation. I noticed that all the debates I saw on social media involved mostly Black people on the side of Trayvon Martin while white people seemed to be on the side of George Zimmerman. To make the matter even much more divisive, 2012 was also an election year.

Barack Obama vs. Mitt Romney.
Black vs. White.
Democrat vs. Republican.

Social media was absolutely exhausting that entire year. Every day, there was a political or a racial debate on the timeline, and seemingly everybody felt the need to defend their stance on every issue. Around that time, I started seeing the phrase "Black Lives Matter" being posted regularly online. That phrase REALLY seemed to get people riled up. I remember my older brother, Lionel, saying to me: "Wow, I didn't realize so many people we went to high school with were so racist."

"The only thing that surprises me is that they are so blind to their own racism," I responded. "No," he replied, "I'm not talking about subliminal racism. They are even using the N-word on their public Facebook statuses."

You could actually feel the weight of this new level of hatred. It was very emotionally, mentally, and physically draining.

Zimmerman was charged with second-degree murder in April 2012, after two months of national protesting and incredible public pressure. The jury eventually found him not guilty in July 2013 due to there being insufficient evidence. A nationwide poll conducted for The Washington Post and ABC News found sharp divisions along racial and political lines over the shooting and over the jury's verdict too. Nearly 90% of African Americans called the shooting unjustified, compared to 33% of whites; and some 62% of Democrats disapproved of the verdict, compared to 20% of Republicans. A week after the verdict, peaceful rallies and vigils were held in more than 100 cities nationwide to protest things such as racial profiling.

In the subsequent years, there have been many public cases of un-armed Black males getting killed by police officers which have led to riots and protests across the country. I remember in 2014, it felt like I was hearing about a new story every other month – Eric Gardner in July 2014, Michael Brown in August 2014, Laquan McDonald in October 2014, and Tamir Rice too in November 2014. My friend James called me that November to try to make sense of it all. James and I met when we went on the mission trip to Kenya together. He was a professional golfer who had gone to one of the most popular universities in the country, in the state of Georgia. During our phone conversation he said: "I really want to get your perspective because you are one of the most well-rounded people I know." I don't remember much about the rest of the conversation, but that was the part that stuck out to me the most because I did not consider myself to be any more well-rounded than most people around me. I remember reflecting on that, then I called him back the next day to offer a counter-thought.

"James, think about this: You went to a university that was predomi-nantly white, played a sport that was dominated by white men, and you are in a profession where older white males have historically oc-cupied most of the space. If you wanted to go an entire day without interacting with a person of a different race, you probably could! It is not that I'm particularly well-rounded, as much as it is that I have had to learn about other cultures by default in order for me to advance. You have had the privilege of not having to think about race."

As of 2019, below is the current distribution of the U.S. population by race and ethnicity:
White: 60.1% (Non-Hispanic)
Hispanic: 18.5%
Black: 12.2%
Asian: 5.6%

Multiple Races: 2.8%
American Indian/Alaska Native: 0.7%
Native Hawaiian/Other Pacific Islander: 0.2%

A Black man who has aspirations to be an executive in corporate America can feel discouraged when they look at the Fortune 500 CEOs. 92.6% of that population in Caucasian. In 2004, there were five Black Fortune 500 CEOs. In 2021? Still five black Fortune 500 CEOs. It doesn't look much better when you look at the rest of the C-level executive positions.

Even in the sports industry, one of my observations in the business is that the higher I looked at organizational and team charts, the less diverse it got. There seemed to be a racial imbalance. The football team I played on in college was made up almost of all Black players. Meanwhile, everyone else—the coaches, the administrators, and the faces in the crowd—were overwhelmingly white. When I would watch the college basketball championship tournament, most of the players on the court—whose sweat and sacrifice made the whole show possible—would be Black. Almost everybody else, from the Head Coaches to the corporate sponsors in the luxury boxes, would not be. The sports industry reminded me of the very same apartheid system that was in South Africa for almost 50 years. Not that people were getting killed or thrown to jail, but there were two sets of rules that created separate classifications of people.

On October 21, 2010, I took the Oath of Allegiance to the United States of America and became a citizen. I remember standing there during the ceremony, processing my experience as a U.S. resident. Honestly, that was around the time I accepted that being Black in America is a continual fight. Fighting for identity, fighting for family, and fighting against institutions and establishments which show us regularly that they will tolerate us, but will still not fully appreciate or accept us.

The American dream is a national ethos based on the idea that anyone can have the opportunity for prosperity and success given they are committed to hard work. As a result, the hard work will then lead to freedom and upward mobility for the family and the children. When you are an immigrant, that dream comes with unimaginable barriers for you to fight through. In any fight, there is a winner and a loser, so why not fight to get the victory?

Like my father, I know that I have to have a good understanding in the classroom but I also know that I need a thorough understanding in life...

There are immigrant minorities across all fifty states who feel stuck within the confines of their neighborhoods. I completely empathize with those who feel oppressed in this country when they try to advance beyond the hood. At the same time, when I think about what my mom and dad had to overcome, I know that the worst hood for someone to be in, is victimhood. There is always hope for one to hold on to. My parents' story is the embodiment of the American Dream as many folks know it.

I remember my dad telling me stories about how whenever his father got paid, he had to hide the money from the rest of the family because if not, it led to arguments with his wives (more about this later) and his kids about how much everyone actually needed. He observed that and made the conscious decision that whenever he married my mom, she would have access to all the financial accounts. It certainly helped that she had a job working at the local bank. When the First Congo War forced our 8-person household out of our home country and eventually out of Africa to North America, we had enough saved up to start a new life because of mom and dad's approach to professionalism.

They left everything that they knew behind, moved to a country where they had no friends, and even had to learn a new language while in their 40's.

My parents chose to go the entrepreneurship route and my mom opened up DACEL Beauty Supplies, a beauty supply shop located in Irving, TX; meanwhile, my dad used his experience in transportation to start a trucking company which was called DBM Trucking. By 2001, three years after arriving in the United States, both my parents were hitting their stride. They ran two businesses, were employing members of the community, and purchased a 5-bedroom home in the suburbs. This is why immigrants come to America: for the meritocracy. If you sow properly and intentionally, then you will reap the rewards. The United States is a capitalist society established with the idea that capitalism promotes and allows for more individual opportunities.

Capitalism, of course, is not a perfect system itself. I'm certainly aware that there are wealthy people who spend their money influencing politicians to tilt the scales of capitalism in their favor, therein leading to income and wealth inequality. Immigrants especially have a love-hate relationship with capitalism because, although it provides opportunity, a good argument can be made about how it has led to exploitation of laborers. More than capitalism, immigrants mostly enjoy the separation of power in the government. The legislative, judicial, and executive branches regulate the abuse of power which so many immigrants are all too familiar with from where they migrate from.

Mom and dad saw nothing but opportunity when they arrived in the United States, despite all the odds being stacked against them… and then… they lost it all, again.

It first started in 2003 when another competing beauty supply shop opened up in the shopping center neighboring my mom's. Owned by Chinese immigrants, this store's prices were so low, that they took nearly all of DACEL's clientele. Less than one year later, my mom had to close her shop and she went out of business. Meanwhile, the United States was at war in the middle east and the operation cost of my dad's trucking company was steadily increasing; especially the oil prices.

To make ends meet, my mom had to take a job where she was stocking and unloading merchandise at Walmart. She started developing back problems at the time, but she didn't have as many work options.

During the time she was working at Walmart, some of my cousins from Paris came to visit us in Texas while they were on vacation. There were three girls in their late teens/early 20's exploring a new country for the first time. When they arrived, my older brother took them on a drive around the Dallas/Fort Worth metroplex to see some sights, and one of the stops was at Walmart so that they could surprise my mom at work. When they met up, they all exchanged hugs and my mother stood there silently in her work uniform.

"I'll see you all when I get home," she said with her chin hanging down. When my brother Lionel saw the look of shame on her, he told me he felt his heart crack.

She had been accustomed to a lifestyle in which my dad made sure that she had a cook, a babysitter, someone to do the household chores, and even a driver when she needed one. She transitioned from having that to doing manual labor in a foreign country, staying up late to

Mom and dad in the 1980's

cook/clean, making sure all the kids were taking care of their school-work, and still being the emotional support for her husband. When the back pain got too serious, she took classes to become a certified nursing assistant, passed the certification, and she started working as a CNA.

When the oil prices spiked in 2005 due to the geopolitical insta-bility in the Middle East, my dad's trucking company was at a net loss. It continued to lose money the following year. When the Great Recession began in 2007, the company could no longer afford to operate. DBM Trucking soon went out of business. My older siblings were relying on federal Pell grants, financial aid, and student loans to attend college. Sometimes, that money was used for day-to-day life instead of for tuition and books. I came to realize years later, that a lot of Americans were not actually living the type of life that they portrayed, even after the recession.

2007 was a humbling year for the Batoba family. That year, my dad flew back and forth between Keller and Kinshasa in search of new career opportunities for himself. Through his connections in the Democratic Republic of Congo he was blessed with the responsibility of overseeing the country's national social security fund in 2008. He learned his lesson not to rely on a single source of income and began investing in commercial and residential real estate in Africa. Fast for-ward to 2021, and my mother works only when she chooses to.

My parents achieved the American dream, then suffered the American nightmare, and then proceeded to remix the original American dream. They achieved the dream of purchasing a residential home in a safe, suburban community where they could raise their children. The nightmare came when they both lost their businesses due to a competitive market and an economic collapse. Their life perspective propelled them forward. Through resiliency, they still have a home in a safe community, children who are college educated, multiple streams of income, and they have opportunities they've created for loved ones in the Democratic Republic of Congo.

The American Dream is no longer about piling up student loan debts in college to find a job that you can work at for 30+ years and contribute to a 401(k), and then retire somewhere in Florida.

My brothers, sisters, and I all consider ourselves unbelievably fortunate to have the parents that we have. Seeing them make the sacrifice of leaving everything they had known behind in order to provide a better life for our family gave me all the perspective I ever needed. Even when it would have been easy to have a victim mentality, they fought to persevere and found a way for them to remix the American Dream.

10

THE LION SPEAKS BACK

DURING MY SENIOR year of college, I decided that I wanted to return to Africa. I knew that my football playing days were over and that I was going to have more free time than I had ever had in my life with no school or sport obligations. Naturally, the first place I looked into going was to the Democratic Republic of Congo. When I talked to my parents about it, my mother didn't think it was the right time due to there being civil unrest after a controversial presidential election.

The previous year, a 30-minute documentary titled *Kony 2012* was released. It was with the intention to draw attention to Joseph Kony, a Ugandan leader of a guerilla group that is responsible for tens of thousands of children being abducted to become child soldiers and sex slaves as well. They were believed to have operated in Uganda, the Democratic Republic of Congo, the Central African Republic, and South Sudan. A poll by the Pew Research Center suggested that more than half of young adult Americans heard about *Kony 2012* in the days following the documentary's release. I was one of those young adults who came across the video and when I watched the people on it speak French, it reminded me of my own family members. I was moved by the film. I didn't want to just go to Africa to visit, but also to serve. I had a deep desire to help.

Since my mom didn't think it was the right time to go, I decided to then look elsewhere. I was involved with an organization in college called Athletes in Action that had a mission trip component. Our campus director, Ian, led me to some resources involving potential mission trips that I could go on after I graduated. I finally made the decision that I would be going to Kenya with other athletes from across the country. On November 5, 2013 I launched an online campaign to raise $4,000 to pay for the whole trip. There was an outpour of support from friends, family, coaches, teachers, and strangers who contributed to the campaign and helped me to raise the necessary funds. I found out that I was going with a group called the College Golf Fellowship – college golfers using the sport to lead people to share the Gospel of Jesus Christ. I didn't know much about golf, but I loved sports and I love Jesus.

We landed in Nairobi, the capital of Kenya, on December 31, 2013. It felt symbolic. I had just finished one chapter of my life a couple of weeks' prior (college) and the year was coming to an end. As the new chapter of life began, along with the New Year, I was returning to the motherland for new blessings in my life to be born.

Nairobi was as incredibly pleasant as its nickname, "The green city in the sun," sounds. The city had flowering trees and perfect climate – sunny with low humidity almost every day. The first thing that stuck out when entering the city was the INTENSE traffic. Cars, motorcycles, buses, and pedestrians were all navigating the streets in what looked like complete chaos, and yet everyone seemed comfortable in it. We made our way to the Great Rift Valley where we played some spontaneous golf with the locals while overlooking breathtaking natural hills, forests, and a volcano. The trip also included a safari where we almost witnessed two lions get into a fight with a pack of hyenas! The camaraderie within our group was great – team Bible studies held by fire at night and group prayers/worship took place regularly.

I was surprised to learn that there are approximately 40 golf courses in the country of Kenya as the sport is growing in popularity. I saw more

Black golfers in Kenya than I had seen in all my years in the United States. We visited numerous clubs, where the group gave some lessons, engaged in conversation, and befriended some aspiring golfers. As the sole football player on the trip, I was also learning about golf and I received plenty of questions about weight-lifting and why I had never tried playing rugby as there were not a lot of muscular people in the city. We met a man named Peter, a Caddy Master at one of the underdeveloped golf courses, who had been running a ministry for caddies for years.

We were able to give him a lot of golf equipment and apparel that were donated for the trip. Most of the courses were well-groomed and the members of the clubs were too. When you meet wealthy people in Kenya, you really see that the wealth is undeniable. Some of these golf courses had luxury cars in the parking lots; other golfers we encountered offered to pay for the entire group to eat delicious meals. Virtually everyone we encountered there was extremely educated, with many of them speaking a minimum of three languages, including English. "Yeah, these darn Americans only speak one language," I would say jokingly as I engaged in French dialogue. It wasn't until a few days into the trip that we really experienced the true reality of Nairobi.

At one of the golf clubs we encountered Jomo, a man who was an orphan and had taught himself how to play golf and caddy. He was from Kibera – a neighborhood in Nairobi that is considered the largest urban slum in all of Africa. A slum is defined as a densely populated area marked by things like crowding, run-down housing, poverty, social disorganization, and a lack of basic services e.g. sanitation, potable water, electricity, etc. Jomo shared with us that he sees it as his life's mission to teach kids in the slums how to play golf and apply golf lessons to life. He especially cares for the refugee children who are there and without any family. After he shared his story with us, we went to the golf course to meet the kids. I met an 11-year-old boy named Abishek who was there with his little sister. He told me that they were from the Democratic Republic of

Congo and his family was split apart when they had to escape from the ongoing Congo war.

They had no idea where their parents were located, but somehow the two of them had made their way out east to Kenya where they lived as refugees, oftentimes staying with Jomo. Abishek was soft-spoken and his little sister was shyly holding his hand as she stood behind him the entire time he talked to me.

They were the sweetest kids.

We found a place on the grass to sit down and talk. Abishek told me about his older brother who was living in South Africa and was trying to become a professional soccer player, but they couldn't get in touch with him. I wanted to encourage them, so I shared my story about fleeing from the Democratic Republic of Congo. I told Abishek and his sister that God had brought them out of their situation because he is not done with them; that God's grace was all over them and that He had greater plans for their lives. I thought to myself "What were the odds that the three of us would meet in Kenya and have this conversation?" The whole interaction felt divine.

The group got back together and we went over a few more golf lessons and we said our goodbyes. As I was walking away, Abishek ran up to me.

"Yves! Yves!" he called out.

I turned around and saw him standing there with a round, bronze medal hanging on a green ribbon. It was very random. On it was written:

LIMURU GOLF FUN DAY
Non-Handicapped
Nearest The Pin

He told me, "I want you to have this. Thank you for sharing your story with me."

He felt like I gave him something of value during our interaction that he too wanted to give me something in return. This kid was unbelievable. I grabbed the medal, thanked him, prayed with him, and gave him a hug. It took everything in me to fight back the tears after I turned around. Even though there were similarities in our journeys, I had my parents, brothers, and sisters with me whenever I left Congo. I cannot imagine going through all of that without them. Later that night, when the group had a debrief of the day, I told them about meeting Abishek and his sister. When I pulled the medal out of my pocket, I couldn't hold all my emotions back anymore. Korky, one of the group leaders, said to me "It's a real emotion. Go ahead and let it out."

I cried my eyes out.

When I wiped my tears away and looked up, I noticed that there wasn't a single dry eye in the group. We decided that we would go visit the Kibera slums during our mission trip. Athletes In Action had a relationship with Soweto Academy, a school in Kibera that was founded in 1988 by the Kenyan Pastor Chris Okumu. In his words, "Education is the most precious gift a nation can give to its children, and a church can give to its members." Just like my father's story, education is often the only means of escape from a cycle of poverty.

The night before we visited Kibera, we gathered as a group and were given a brief history of the area and a run-down of what we were to expect:

- Extreme poverty (most people earn less than $1.00 per day)
- High unemployment rates
- Many people living with HIV
- A strong sense of community
- Friendly attitudes
- Uncommon joy

These things kind of seemed contradicting, but anyway okay. It was a Sunday afternoon when we arrived in Kibera and met with the man who was to be our guide through the slums. People had just gotten out of church and were dressed in their Sunday best. Our guide told us, "The people take a lot of pride in looking good, especially when they own a suit." Despite the hot weather outside, I saw plenty of men wearing suits and wearing them with dignity too. It reminded me of what my mom told me about my dad when they met: even though he did not come from much, he always made sure that he was present-able in appearance.

As we walked on the streets which were covered in dirt, we were in the middle of hyperactivity. Residents were outside frying fish, chopping vegetables, running around with soccer balls at their feet, selling goods and products, or just simply gathering with neighbors. The living quarters were separated by thin pieces of tin and it wasn't unusual to see as many as 6 people inhabiting a space of less than 100 square feet. We saw some stray chickens running around the streets and the occasional dog roaming freely. It took a while for us to get ourselves over the initial shock of just how many people were packed into such a small area. The size of Kibera is approximately just 1 square mile but with a dense population greater than 200,000 people. Talk about heartbreaking. A few of the kids who attended Soweto Academy Junior saw us as we were walking up and they ran up to us with excitement. One of the boys jumped right into my arms and I carried him as we got a tour of the school. The students' uniforms consisted of a collared shirt worn under a purple sweater. The girls wore long, lavender skirts and the boys wore plum-colored shorts or pants.

We played games with the kids, shared a lot of laughs, and they also wanted to take a lot of pictures. The happiness on their faces was priceless! We met the school's principal, Johnstone, who shared his vision for the school: "We pray that these children are the ones who will grow up and form the government here. Because they are ne-glected people, and when you are neglected you see that the people doing well do not mind that you are in trouble." He took us to a water pump near the school that was actually built by the Athletes In Action ministry a few years before our own group arrived. They purify the water at the distillery where it has been tested and is some of the purest drinking water in all of Kenya. They bottle the water to sell it and raise money for the school, but since it comes from Kibera, they have a hard time selling it. Even if something good comes out of Kibera, it'll be judged first by the negative stigmas.

When we left the worst poverty we had ever seen in our lives in Kibera, our group went back to our comfortable, gated residence complete with plumbing and electricity.

That's life in Africa. Wealth and poverty – without much in the middle.

With some of the boys at Soweto Academy in Kibera.

There is a lot of beauty in Africa that we are not normally exposed to in the United States. Maybe if it was more prominent, there would be a greater desire for people to travel to the motherland and visit. The reality however, is that the poverty far outweighs the wealth in Africa. Before I went on the mission trip to Kenya, I spoke to several people who had done mission trips in the past and they would frequently say something along the lines of "They're so happy even in their poor circumstances" or "I was actually kind of jealous of how much joy they had." I couldn't quite put my finger on it, but something about statements like those did not sit right with me.

Most of our group went on a golf tournament the following day and part of us went back to the Kibera slums to have deeper interactions. We walked back to Soweto Academy and met with some school officials who took us into some classrooms where the kids sang songs for us and recited Bible scriptures. Korky and I were asked to speak to a classroom of girls about what kind of qualities to look for in God-fearing men. These girls expressed desires to eventually be married, but great discernment is needed because of the amount of violence against girls in the area. Some of the girls were attentive and happy to see us, but I noticed that a few of them rolled their eyes at what we had to say. "Don't take it personal," one of the teachers told me. "They have been badly hurt."

It is hard not to feel helpless.

I remembered those statements about "How happy they are," so I started asking the adults questions about where the happiness comes from in Kibera. After numerous 1-on-1 conversations, I realized that there is often a tendency to romanticize the happiness of the poor. The people who go on mission trips forget that their presence might be the distraction that makes things bearable for the locals while they are with them for an hour or so. Anybody who is in a low-income area has the capacity to laugh, whether they are in Texas or in Kibera. But when you live in that low quality of life, and you do have moments of pleasure, you ensure to enjoy them to the fullest. Moments of happiness become so rare and precious that you have to stop yourself and really treasure them.

One of the locals I sparked a conversation with said, "Every day we don't know how we are going to survive. We don't know where our food is going to come from. But we pray and the LORD provides."

When I returned to the United States in late January 2014, I took the medal given to me by Abishek out of my bag and hung it around my car's rear view mirror. As I reflected on my mission trip to Africa, this old African proverb came to mind:

"Until the lion learns how to write, every story will glorify the hunter."

Any time I had heard from Americans who went on mission trips to Africa, I only heard about their experiences, most of which painted a false picture of a "happiness" existing in these dangerously impoverished parts of the continent. The reality that I came to discover from actually having conversations with those living in the slums (a.k.a. the lions), is that there are real bureaucratic and financial incentives for why infamously powerful people (a.k.a. the hunters) keep them in those same oppressive conditions. Until the oppressed and the hunted is given a voice to genuinely articulate their story, the narrative of the oppressor and hunter will remain dominant.

One of the things that struck me in the slums was the real appreciation that people have for the things that are not hard, the things that brought about laughter. Neighbors were helping each other clean and feed each other's families. It just seemed like there was a real understanding that they were going through a difficult life, but it is better they did it together and truly connected as human beings. In the Western world, there is an obsession with the pursuit of happiness and fulfillment. What I really admire about the people of Kibera, is not their happiness. It's being able to face the drudgery in the world and find a way for it to be the beginning of the story and not for it to be the end. Not just once, but over and over again. Despite all of the misdeeds that are constantly thrown at the lion, that lion ensures to carry on. That daily capacity is incredibly moving.

One day, after a couple of months had passed, my friend Hailey got in my car and noticed the medal hanging in the middle of the windshield. "What's this about?" I was glad she asked and was excited to tell her the story. So I began to tell her about Abishek and the day we met at the golf course. In the middle of the story, I paused. I caught myself about to cry again the same way that I did when I was in Kenya. "It's okay," said Hailey. I recomposed myself and finished the story. "It reminds me of the importance of human connection," I continued to her. "Perspective is a powerful thing to gain. Sometimes you only get it by listening to someone's story, and I realize that I don't have to go all the way to Kenya to gain real perspective."

Perhaps the biggest perspective that I needed to gain was one from my family's perspective. My brothers, sisters, and I were not raised to be very vulnerable or to share our feelings and emotions. In fact, the words "I love you" were hardly ever said in our household; maybe occasionally on a birthday or before someone boarded a flight. That year, 2014, I decided to make an effort to use "I love you" more with members of my family. I started by testing it out on phone calls. Right before I would hang up, it felt like saying word vomit.

"OKAYILOVEYOUBYE."

I had to ease my way into this! It was new. After a few times of saying "OKAYILOVEYOUBYE" at the end of phone conversations, I graduated to saying "LOVE YOU…" and then I'll wait for a response. The first time I remember hearing "love you too" was at the end of a call with Lionel, my older brother. Shortly after, my little sister, Laetitia, started saying it; followed closely by my mother. I remember visiting my sister, Patricia, and her husband, Allan, at their house and saying it in person when it was time to leave.

As I went in to give Patricia a hug, I said "Okay, I'll see y'all later. Love you."

She responded, "Yeah, thanks for coming. We'll see you soon. Bye!"

It wasn't completely comfortable for everyone yet, and especially not in person, but we were on a roll! In the beginning of that summer, I received a phone call from the University of Notre Dame, saying that I had been offered a job in their athletic department.

When I called my dad over the phone to tell him that I had accepted the role, he said "I'm really proud of you. I love you." I was 23 years old and it was the first time I recalled him saying that to me outside of a birthday. I always knew that my dad loved me... but it felt good hearing it, too. It just felt important to say. It wasn't long until I started hearing everyone in my family saying it to each other more often. These days, it is not as rare.

Before I married my wife, Dawn, she once told me "It seems like your family is really close. I'm kind of jealous of your group chat because it's always cracking you up." It took years of work for us to get to that point. Dawn never saw the times that Lionel and I went 4+ years of hardly saying anything to each other. She didn't know that Laetitia didn't feel like she could trust any of her siblings because, quite frankly, we all betrayed her trust and didn't even realize it. There were times too that Nathan felt neglected and Patricia didn't feel supported. My oldest sister, Lydie, got married, moved to Virginia and we went a decade without seeing her as well. I have another brother, Davister, who I didn't even know about until he was 11 years old.

Every family has its dirty laundry, but there is a strong stereotype that African households are absurdly strict, authoritative, and that they also lack empathy and compassion. Here are ten basic stereotypes of growing up in an African household:

- You learn to be passive aggressive. Why? Because voicing your real aggressions will have severe ramifications. Grumbling internally becomes your greatest skill.

- From ages 0–20, you're dead if they see you with the opposite sex. If you're a woman, though, you'll start getting queries about whether you've found a husband or not at 21 years old.
- The sex talk consists of "You're going to hell if you have sex before marriage."
- If you're not top of your class, you're failing at life.
- Your feelings don't matter because you'll always be: "just a child."
- Your parents are the most dramatic people ever. Situations go from 0 to 100 really quickly. You didn't do the dishes? You might as well have joined a gang and sold your soul to the devil.
- Anything you've done wrong gets broadcasted to 1 million relatives who will want to talk to you to voice their disappointment.
- To balance the previous point, the good things will also make sure to get broadcasted so that the aunties who have underachieving children get jealous.
- 90% of your opinions are probably going to be dismissed as liberal nonsense.
- You tend to think carefully about your actions because you know corporal punishment would be awaiting you at home.

My parents are lovely and I love them very much. In my adulthood, I'm largely grateful for how I was brought up and I hold them in high esteem for how they too have evolved in matters dealing with their children. Although most of those aforementioned stereotypes apply to them too, they evolved into some of the most open-minded African parents that I have ever been around, and that sincerely deserves a lot of credit considering the poor examples they were given.

What Dawn and other people are witnessing when they see us laughing and getting along is the result of prayer, therapy, forgiveness, and healing. When I started thinking about marriage and starting my own family, I made it a point to have more intentional conversations with my parents concerning marriage. While I was busy thinking about giving a voice to the lions in Africa, I overlooked the lion pride which I grew up with. What I have learned from my parents and my siblings made me realize that I really didn't know anything at all.

11

THE DAWN OF YVES

ON THE MORNING of January 28, 2017 I picked up my phone to make two phone calls. The first one was to my big sister, Patricia, and it was to wish her a happy birthday. Three years prior, she almost lost her life. When Patricia and Allan were expecting their first child in 2014, there were pregnancy complications due to her having lupus. The doctors gave her and their daughter, Maddison, less than a 15% chance to survive. She writes about this in her book *A Miracle in the Making: A Journey of Faith, Hope, and Love*. Thinking about the mortality of someone you love dearly is tremendously sobering. I believe that it was the birth of Maddie that really showed our family how precious life is and that it was okay for us to be vulnerable with one another.

The second phone call I made that morning was to my mom and dad; it was their 33rd marriage anniversary. Yes, Patricia's birthday shares the same date.

"Happy anniversary, Mami and Papa!" I said as they answered the phone. Every time I speak to my parents, I do so in French. I don't get too many opportunities to have dialogue in French anymore, so I always take advantage of it when I talk to my parents and they are also quick to correct me if I say something incorrectly. While I had them both on the phone, I asked "What's the secret to being married for

33 years?" What proceeded was about 30 minutes of lecturing, but I was taking notes as they spoke and jotted down the four main points which were mentioned.

The secret to 33 years of marriage:

- Patience to know one another. Because the two of you are always growing.
- Forgiveness for when they let you down. Because nobody is perfect and they WILL let you down.
- Financial stability. Because your relationship is a lot better when you don't have to stress about money.
- Keep God as the foundation. Because He provides the spirit of love.

From the outside looking in, it is nothing short of a miracle that my parents have made it as far as they have. My father grew up in a household where his dad had multiple wives. Polygamy tends to normalize the idea that women are to be subordinate possessions of men who are to be plurally collected to add to a man's glory. These polyamorous relationships are still very common in different parts of Africa. My dad, in particular, knew that he would only want a single wife; something that is not as easy as it may sound considering when the environment does not necessarily value faithfulness in marriage.

My mom had to have a lot of forbearance towards the beginning of her relationship with my dad, because she understood the environment he came from. He had friends and even family members that were introducing other women to him even WHILE HE WAS MARRIED. I don't know what our lives would have been like if we would have never left Kinshasa, but I do know that a man's flesh is weak and that he can only be tempted for so long. Oftentimes, the people who were introducing these women to my dad were doing so with selfish intent, so that the new woman could convince my dad to give them some money. As the great theologian C.S. Lewis once said, "Only those who try to resist temptation know how strong it is." Our entire family dynamic may have been completely different had we not moved to America, where polygamy is largely frowned upon.

My parents always made sure that we had all of our basic needs, that we were polite, and that we also had proper etiquette. We were raised to be respectful of others, and especially obedient of our parents. Sometimes to the point where we even feared them. There were times when we would hear my dad come home from work and we would quickly flee from the living room and all common areas, just so that we didn't risk accidentally angering him and being disciplined because of it. I've had plenty of conversations with friends of mine who are Congolese and they said they used to do the same thing. It was the norm. It wasn't until I started going to my friends' houses in America that I saw a different type of parent-child interaction. I had some white friends who did all but curse their parents out.

At 11 years old, I was hanging out at my friend Walker's house and his dad barged into his room and asked him if he had used his fax machine. "Yeah, I had to send someone this drawing I did," he said to him with a snarky tone.

"Well don't use it anymore without my permission," his dad replied. "What?! Why not? If I have something I want to send, I'm just going to use it!"

When Walker said this, I prepared myself for all hell to break loose. I just knew his dad was going to march up and to slap him silly. Instead, his dad looked at me and said "Sorry, Yves, but you have to go home. Walker is now GROUNDED."

"No, Yves is not going anywhere," Walker said as he stared dead into his father's eyes. That was my cue to put my shoes on and get out of that house. I could not believe the disrespect I had just witnessed. Never in my life had I even heard of a kid talking to his parents that way. I walked back home and I thought to myself, "What the heck is being GROUNDED? The only 'grounded' I know of is being on the ground trying to catch the belt as I'm getting hit by it."

I thought these white Americans kids were out of their minds. From my point of view, my parents were strict, but were easy-going. As long as I was respectful, took care of my grades, and didn't get caught fighting or sneaking out of the house, they would let me hang out with my friends, which was what I mostly cared about then. I now realize just how naive I was as the middle child who spent a lot of time outside of the house and did not pay attention to the experiences of my other brothers and sisters. Depending on which one of us you ask, you'll get different responses about the type of parenting we received.

There was a time I drove to pick up a friend, who also grew up in a Congolese household. She asked me to go to the gym with her so that I could help her put a fitness plan together. When I got to her house, I remember standing in her living room and meeting her brother, sisters, and her parents as they were all in the middle of a board game. While I waited for her to get ready, I observed their interaction with each other – it was full of laughter, high fives, and fun. Before she walked out of the front door, she gave each of her parents a hug and a kiss.

"You don't really see much of that in an African household," I said to her as we got in my car.

"See much of what?" she asked.

"I don't know… The whole vibe in there was very nice. It seems like you all really enjoy each other."

"Oh! Yeah. I think it is because my mom and dad got a Marriage Counselor when they moved to America. They unpacked a lot of things and they talked about parenting there, too. I think that has really helped us as a family."

Africans seeing a counselor. I had never even heard of it. There is already a stigma that exists in the Black American community, but it is not even discussed in the Black African community. My parents haven't gone to a formal counseling session, but Patricia might as well be our own family therapist, as she is a licensed social worker and therapist. She could have probably retired off of our family alone if she charged us for the amount of times we went to her in order to talk things through.

As I reflected on that conversation in the car when I was in my mid-twenties, it made me realize that I knew my parents only as parents, but I did not know them very well as people. I talked to Lionel about it and he said he actually had the same realization and decided one day to take my dad to a bar, buy two beers, and just talk about life, careers, relationships, upbringing, and whatever else came to his mind. What a great idea. When he told me that, I decided to do the same thing. I was particularly curious about mom and dad's marriage. I thought back to the "Secrets to 33 years of marriage," and wanted to ask about number 2: Forgiveness for when they let you down, because they will let you down.

Except that I wanted to connect with them back home. In the Democratic Republic of Congo.

I had expressed to my mom before that I wanted to go visit, but she always had a reason to be worried. Even though she had gone back plenty of times, she insisted that it was different for her than it is for us. If there is one thing I know about my mom, it is that she is going to worry about her kids. Especially when we bring up visiting Congo. Her reasons for worrying included:

- "The timing is not right."
- "The elections are going on and there is a civil uprising."
- "There is too much witchcraft."
- "People might try to harm you."

Way too many excuses! So in early 2018, I went against what she had always taught me about obeying parents and I bought myself a flight to Congo. I didn't know what kind of travel requirements were needed or what my mom would think, but I figured that if I just bought a non-refundable ticket and bought it months in advance, there would be no excuses to go back. I would get the travel requirements done and my mom would have plenty of time to accept that I'm going to Congo.

"Wow," she said when I told her. "Wow wow wow... this could be good." Surprisingly, she took the news well. Any worry that she and my dad may have previously had suddenly turned into excitement for them. After twenty years after leaving the country, I was actually going back to my birthplace. But first, I had to find an engagement ring so that I could propose to my girlfriend.

Dawn and I met on the 24th of June 2016 in Miami, FL. A mutual friend of ours, David, was throwing a get-together at his high-rise apartment and had invited a number of people to come over. My best friend, Elliott, was in town and he tagged along with me at David's place. As people were coming in, I recognized most of them from church. When I saw Dawn walk through the door, I remember saying to myself, "She looks a lot like Kelly Rowland." David introduced us and we sparked up a conversation.
"I just moved to Miami about a week ago," she said.
"Oh yeah? Where from?" I asked.
"Well, I'm from California but I was living in Tulsa, Oklahoma right before I came here."
"Good ol' Oklahoma. I went to school there. What brought you to Miami?"

She proceeded to tell me about how she and her girlfriends wanted to take a girls trip to somewhere where they had never been before. They decided on Miami. While they were on the trip, her best friend told the group that there was a church she heard of which she really wanted to visit on Sunday morning. "I did not want to go to church while on vacation, but Fatima insisted."

"Wait a minute," I interrupted. "I know a girl in Tulsa named Fatima. Are we talking about the same person?" So she pulled up her Instagram page and we saw that her best friend was the same girl I went to school with at Oklahoma State. So we video called Fatima on FaceTime and told her about how we met and how small of a world it was. As the night went on, we discussed other friends in common from Oklahoma and what life in Miami was like. She had a boyfriend and I too had a girlfriend at the time, so we were not interested in each other beyond our conversations that night. As Elliott and I were leaving, I said to him "You know, that Dawn girl was pretty dang cool." I saw her again a couple of days later at church, where we greeted each other and shared some laughs. I would see her again on July 4th, where another mutual friend was throwing a party, and then on most Sundays when she was serving at church.

By the middle of July, my girlfriend and I had broken up. Things were about to ramp back up at work with the Miami Dolphins, which meant that I wouldn't have much time for church or a social life, so I shifted my focus to that. When Training Camps begin across the NFL in late July, there is usually not much time for interaction with any-one outside of the facilities for about four weeks. Things slow down a little when the football season begins in August, but not so much. That year was different, as a massive hurricane was developing near the Atlantic coast of the United States. During football season, we were monitoring the storm closely and were forced to take some days off of practice in case we had to evacuate. During one of those off days, I remember logging onto Facebook to see Dawn evacuating from Florida to Oklahoma.

I sent her a message, jokingly saying "Go be free. The world needs Kelly Rowland." That led to a brief exchange where we somehow started talking about taco places in Oklahoma. I told her, "When you come back I have to take you to this taco spot in Fort Lauderdale." She agreed. Thankfully, the hurricane missed us in South Florida and when she returned, I picked her up at her place and took her out to eat at Rocco's Tacos near downtown Fort Lauderdale.

During dinner, she finished her story about why she moved to Florida. "When we went to church that day while on vacation, I just kept hearing God tell me that this was home. I kept hearing the word 'HOME' after that." I was so intrigued by how spiritually in tune she was. When she returned to Oklahoma from vacation, she stayed in prayer about what she had heard in Miami. She told me, "It didn't make any sense. Why would I move to Miami where I don't know anyone and don't even have a job lined up or anything? But I did it. I packed everything up and moved to Miami just over three months later."

After listening to her story, I paid for our dinner and took her back home. As I was driving back to my place, I reflected on her story of faith and it just made me so much more interested in her. I wanted to know about her upbringing, her hobbies, and her goals. So I went home and typed up a specific, deliberate, thought-out list of questions on my phone. I came up with over 20 questions of things that I wanted to know about her. I was told growing up that I should be very intentional in figuring out who a woman is if I'm interested in her. That it's not something to take lightly, because your life partner is the most important decision you make after your faith. My plan was to bring all of these questions up organically through our conversations over time. What actually happened was I asked them all in one night.

The second time that the two of us were together was at her place and we talked for over three hours. Every question I had came up, and by the time I was walking out of the door I thought to myself, "She's the one for me." Years after we got married, I asked her what she thought about that night and she told me that she felt uncomfortable having to talk so much about herself, because no guy had ever asked her questions like that. We met on June 24, 2016, shared our first kiss on June 24, 2017, and we got engaged on June 24, 2018 when I proposed to her in front of her family and friends during a game night. I knew she was the one I wanted to spend my life with, and I knew that I wasn't just marrying her but marrying into her entire family. My mom used to tell me to not just pray for my future wife, but to also pray for her family for this very reason.

Members of my family and Dawn's family
celebrating our engagement

Being in a relationship with Dawn felt like my life was really beginning. It was the "Dawn of Yves," if you will. She brought more beauty and new meaning to my life. I knew that marriage would take real work, especially when combining worlds. In our unique situation, our marriage was also going to be an intercultural one.

My life experience introduced me to families of a lot of different cultures. Whether it be because of different social classes, different races, or different ethnicities, my cross-cultural capacity is high because of lived interactions and friendships. Even though I had a good understanding of Congolese culture from being around Congolese people in America, I knew that that did not compare to physically being in the Democratic Republic of Congo. I wanted to learn about our authentic heritage and traditions. I wanted to hold on to the lessons about marriage and to steer clear of the mistakes, because not all traditions are good traditions. So eight days after I got engaged, I boarded a flight to go back to Africa. This time, it was to go back to the Congo.

12

INTERCULTURAL LOVE

MY VOYAGE TO Congo felt like I was going on two trips, because I had a 24-hour layover in Dubai on the way there, and then a 23-hour layover on the way back. Dubai is a country I've never been to, but I had heard a lot about it in recent years. I did some research on the airplane and read up on how liberal it is compared to the seven Emirates. Though it is still an Arab Emirate with a large Islam influence. I had to read up on what not to do, so I didn't get myself in any trouble. No criticizing the royal family, local laws, or the country in general. No drinking in public, no exposed knees or shoulders seen in public spaces. Very different from what I was accustomed to in the United States, but in just over 20 years, Dubai has transformed into the most luxurious city in the world.

When I landed at the Dubai International Airport, there was a sign that read "WORLD'S FASTEST WI-FI" just inside my terminal. Of course I had to test it out. I took out my phone and connected to the wi-fi and I couldn't believe just how much speed it had, especially for a free public airport. As I was leaving the airport, I purchased a one-day metro ticket and set out on my quest to explore as much of the city as I could before my flight back to Congo. My 23 hours in Dubai were nothing short of extraordinary; the world's tallest building, the world's largest mall, beautiful artificial islands, man-made marinas, luxury uber rides, and an incredible water show at the Dubai Fountain.

While I was walking through the Gold Souk, I heard a call to prayer and every shop and restaurant stopped their music/entertainment to allow the locals to pray. There was something special about being in such a futuristic city which still honored their traditions.

When I returned to the airport after a day of exploring, I was even more excited to go back to Congo. I thought to myself, "If Dubai had this type of transformation in about 20 years, I wonder what Kinshasa has been like since I left 20 years ago." My stay in Kinshasa was scheduled for ten days and I wanted to maximize every minute of it. Upon landing at the N'djili International Airport, I quickly realized that my experience in Kinshasa wasn't going to be anything like Dubai. There was the lack of infrastructure, technology, and organized systems at the airport that gave off a careless first impression. Almost as if they don't care how anyone perceived the country as they entered it. Making it from the airplane to being greeted by my family on the other side required navigating a lot of chaos from the middle.

I was met by mom, dad, and my half-brother, Davister. I was 26 years old, Davister was 19, and it was our first time meeting in person. We had spoken over the phone numerous times and we were both eager for each other to finally connect. "He kept telling everyone that he can't wait to meet his big brother," my mom told me. There was so much I wanted to know about his upbringing in Kinshasa; I felt like it would give me an idea of how I may have turned out if I had lived there. With every conversation, I learned that Davister is a deep thinker and a charmer who, like my father, is book smart and street smart. He knew how to navigate his way around the city and how to communicate with just about anybody.

As we drove into the property that my dad purchased and finished building in 2014, I was astonished. The big, white house with its modern design immediately demands your attention when you enter the front gate. We drove down a long driveway with beautiful landscaping on each side that curved around the lot into a three-car garage. Beside the garage, there was a walkway that led to the pool house and swimming pool. My parents and Davister took me on a tour around the house – 8 bedrooms, 8.5 bathrooms, 2 living rooms, 2 dining rooms, 1 office, 1 prayer room, 1 basement, with balconies all around the house. The pool house was also stocked with a full bar and a great sound system. They had a cook, gardener, guards, a driver, and other people who came by to do miscellaneous work. My folks were living like royalty.

Every day that I was in Congo, cousins, uncles, aunties, and friends of the family came to the house to visit. "I cannot believe it. You are actually here!" I heard these words often, along with "Last time I saw you, you were so small" and "I did not expect you to still know so much French! Do you speak Lingala, too?" I didn't speak Lingala, but I could understand it. What I was always cognizant of was them knowing that I was not different or separated, other than by distance. It was important to me that they know, but it was important for me to know, too. Even though I spent most of my life in the United States, I always had a connection to Congo and had a strong desire to return. That includes returning to my old elementary school, the house we lived in before we evacuated, and the building my dad used to work in. As I got in the car to be driven to these places, I couldn't help but feel very saddened and discouraged. Everything looked worse 20 years later than it did when we left.

The house I lived in used to have big, beautiful flowers outside of the property; all of that had turned into dirt. There was a new family living there now and the walls on the outside were also deteriorating. Even the road right outside of the house was cracked and deteriorated by massive potholes. "This country has been headed in the opposite direction of Dubai," I thought to myself. The infrastructure of everything that I recognized growing up has become more regressive, and meanwhile the population density has gotten so dense that it is hard to get an accurate number of inhabitants in the city. It is somewhere between 8 million and 20 million. The visual alone was maddening. It felt like the very government had forgotten its citizens.

When we went to my late grandparents' houses, I was greeted by cousins who I had never met. It felt surreal looking around in there and remembering the times I sat on the front steps and laughed at my grandfather's jokes as a kid. Like the rest of what I saw, the houses also looked old and rotten. Everywhere I looked, I saw street vendors selling anything and everything. Water, soda, bread, cell phone chargers, toys, and more.

"Be alert and pay attention when you are out because there are a lot of thieves," my mother warned me as Davister and I set out to walk around. There was never a moment that I felt threatened. Part of that may just be because there is no threat of gun violence. Even as people would yell as they communicated with one another, I understood that it was all just a part of Congolese culture. We are a very loud and expressive group of people. Davister and I met up with some of his friends, who knew all about me, for some bowling inside of Le Premier Shopping Mall. This was the first mall built in Kinshasa and was one of the most developed buildings I had stepped foot in during my visit, resembling any regular mall you would find in the United States. After a full day of touring, the driver picked us up and we returned back home, where I told my parents about how disheartening it was to see how much everything has regressed.

But that's life in Congo. If you have money, you can live well. If you are struggling to get ahead, don't expect the government to roll out any social programs. I thought about how beneficial a welfare government program would be for my widowed aunt and her six kids who all lived in a house with no running water. Things such as food stamps and section 8 housing that exist in the United States would be seen as a luxury in Congo. "People here are not living," my father said. "They are simply surviving." This was a big reason why mom and dad always opened their doors to friends/family, and are always willing to host a celebration.

During my visit, mom and dad threw a huge celebration at the house. It felt like everyone was in Congo. I met uncles who I had been communicating with online for years. "We drove 2 hours to come here and see you," they said to me. I felt like the prodigal son who had returned or something. "Now when you go back, you can tell the rest of the family that it is not so scary. Bring them and your fiancé back next time." What a blessing it was to be back with my family. It was the first time in my life that I had ever been around that much family and I definitely did not want it to be my last.

During my last day in Congo, as we drove through the city one last time before I had to go to the airport, I couldn't help but notice the energy present in the city. The bars were always playing music and people were dancing seemingly in every neighborhood. I said to my dad, "One thing about Congolese people is that we're going to find a way to dance and have fun." He responded with, "Why do you think Kinshasa is so known for its music and dances? Life is hard! We have to find a way to create our own ambience."

Those words stuck with me.

It's great to have hope for the future, but it's more important to have hope just for the day. Just enough faith, hope, and love for that day. Congolese people are people who create our own ambience. The entire decision to buy the flight ticket was me "creating my own ambience." Things may be chaotic and uncertain around me, but I must dance to my own music in order to stay sane. When I boarded that flight out of the Congo with a 24-hour layover in Dubai, I felt more connected to my identity than I had ever felt. Less than one year later, on the 23rd of March 2019, Dawn and I got married by the beach at the W Fort Lauderdale hotel.

Our wedding ceremony was traditionally American, whereas our wedding reception required us to change into African-print fabric from Congo which were tailored into modern-looking ankaras. Our wedding guests were Immigrants and Americans. We played R&B music AND Congolese Soukous music. We had created our own ambience in our intercultural love.

During the "money dance" portion of our wedding after the outfit change

*Marrying Dawn is easily one of the best things
to ever happen to the Batoba family*

The more time Dawn spent around my family, the more she wanted to learn about her ethnic roots. There was a time during our honeymoon, when she met some of my family members who lived in France and they asked her where she was from. She told them, "I'm from California." They said, "No, where are you from originally? Before California." She looked at me and she didn't know what to tell them. We just laughed and said "We don't know yet, but we'll find out." That following Christmas, I got her an ancestry test kit which traced a large percentage of her DNA back to Nigeria, Cameroon, Congo & Southern Bantu Peoples.

Dawn and I love to explore, so naturally, we also began planning for a trip to the Democratic Republic of Congo in 2020. The global pandemic prevented us from doing much traveling that year, but it turned out to be a blessing in disguise because it allowed for the rest of my siblings to plan for a family trip in 2021. On May 24, I boarded a flight with Dawn and my little brother, Nathan, from Dallas to Los Angeles. In Los Angeles, we stayed with Lionel at his loft and we spent a couple of days exploring the city with him. He then joined us as we boarded another flight at midnight on May 26 for New York, where we met up with my little sister, Laetitia, at her apartment in the Washington Heights neighborhood. At each stop, we had just enough layover time to tour some great landmarks before our next flight. After New York, the five of us finally left for our overseas flight. My parents were already in Congo expecting our arrival.

Getting to that point of the trip felt like a miracle in itself, due to all the obstacles that were in our way. Because of the COVID-19 virus, we wanted to ensure that we were all fully vaccinated, and then we each had to have routine travel vaccines for Congo (Yellow Fever, malaria, hepatitis A, etc.). Nathan and Laetitia almost couldn't get their routine travel vaccines because of some scheduling issues. Then out of nowhere, one week before we were supposed to leave, the passport office informed Nathan that his application to renew his passport was denied, even though he had submitted it months in advance. Although we were able to get everything resolved, it felt like there was some type of mystic opposition against us going on this trip together.

This return to our homeland was long overdue. We all knew it and at a spiritual level, we believe that the devil also knew it and wanted to prevent it from happening. We had multiple prayer meetings as a family to be in agreement for smooth travels, patience, and resiliency. We needed all of those things.

When we arrived at the N'Djili International Airport in Kinshasa, I was so excited to be there with my family. I was mostly just staying back and watching their reactions to everything. I knew that the airport experience would be overwhelming for them and I was right. We were crammed in a room with other travelers to go through COVID-19 testing protocols that took way too long. It all seemed very counterproductive. When we went to the parking lot to meet my parents, we were bombarded with people who were offering to help carry our bags, load up the vehicles, and anything else that they could do so that we could give them a tip.

God bless my mother, who always wanted to stay a little longer to make sure that everyone who helped us received some money. At first, it would be easy for anyone to feel afraid when getting approached by so many people at once. But then you realize that no one will do any harm. They just want to provide some type of value so that they could get compensated for it.

"This is what happens when you are desperate," Lionel said. "Unfortunately there is a shortage of jobs, infrastructure is lacking, and there are no social programs by the government. This is what desperation looks like."

The first night we were in town, we went to visit a friend of the family at her home where the electricity was out in the entire neighborhood. They had gone about three days without any electricity up until that point. With no city lights around, it was pitch black as she greeted us with enormous excitement in her voice. "The Batoba family is back home! I have gifts for everybody!" This time around in Congo, there was a whole itinerary planned out: We attended my cousin's wedding, we experienced the nightlife in the city, we had a meeting with a local pastor who had been friends with our parents for over a decade so he could pray and prophesy over us, and we planned to visit the Congo River. The same river that my siblings and I had to cross 24 years earlier in order to save our lives.

Being at the Congo River that day was a completely surreal feeling.

Uncle Para and Aunt Louise rode to the river with us, along with my cousin, Erudit, who had also escaped with us that day. I stood there on the edge of the water, looking out at the old boats where fishermen were working. Boats that still looked the exact same way as I remembered them. I was overcome with gratitude as I looked across the river onto Brazzaville, the capital of our neighboring country, the Republic of Congo. The last time I was in Brazzaville was in 1997 when I was watching cartoons in a dark living room with my siblings, cousins, aunt, and uncle. I vividly remember watching The Mask: Animated Series while we could hear the assault rifles and explosions outside.

I just remember the adults talking about the escape plan with another man who was there to guide us. "Every time I yell 'EARTH' you all have to go to the ground. When I yell 'STAND' you have to get up and keep running."

All the memories rushed back. To have that moment with my arm wrapped around my wife brought to me immense gratitude and appreciation of life. I looked around and saw my little brother taking photos with his cousins whom he had never met before. I looked up at the sky and whispered, "Thank you, God, for protection and redemption." After surviving what we survived, there had never been a moment in my life where I didn't feel like each person in my family wasn't here on purpose for a purpose.

A few days into our trip, Davister flew in from South Africa, where he was attending college. This was everyone else's first time meeting their brother in person. Davister and Nathan had been messaging each other for weeks leading up to the trip, so watching them interact and hit it off right away was heartwarming; the two youngest Batobas. Later that evening, Patricia and Allan surprised the rest of the family by showing up at the house unannounced. All along, everyone thought they were in Texas because they couldn't find a babysitter for Maddison, but Allan's mom agreed to watch her and Dawn and I were helping them plan their travels so that they too could surprise everyone.

We were all there. So naturally, my parents threw another party.

At this party I met Yvette, my mother's best friend from her younger days who she thought she would name her unborn daughter after. Instead, she was pregnant with a boy and named him Yves instead. I never even knew this story, but I met my namesake that night. These are talking points that sometimes come up when the environment calls for it. I found great pleasure in watching my mom introduce my siblings to distant family members whom they never met, or re-introduce them because they hadn't seen each other in 23 years. After a night of dancing, laughing, eating, and drinking, my mother received a phone call the next morning from my oldest sister, Lydie. Unbeknownst to any of us, she also landed in Kinshasa the night of the party, along with her husband and four daughters.

It had been over a decade since the last time I saw Lydie, but she told my mother that she wanted to come by the house and see everyone. Before we could even finish our food while we were at the breakfast table talking about it, we saw them pull up into the driveway. All of us had not been together in Congo since 1999 and here we all were. We all gathered in the living room and shared laughs before we broke into worship and a family prayer, just like we used to do while growing up. I looked up as everyone was in prayer and scanned the room. I just needed to immortalize that moment in my memory.

The Immigrant Americans had come full circle.

Reunited in Kinshasa for the first time in about 23 years

CPSIA information can be obtained
at www.ICGtesting.com
Printed in the USA
BVHW081102151221
624011BV00012B/1093